Charles Olson & Ezra Pound

Also by Charles Olson

Call Me Ishmael
The Maximus Poems
Human Universe and Other Essays
Selected Writings
Maximus Poems IV, V, VI
Pleistocene Man
Causal Mythology
Archaeologist of Morning
The Special View of History
Letters for *Origin* 1950–1956
Poetry and Truth
Additional Prose
The Post Office
The Maximus Poems: Volume Three

Charles Olson

&

Ezra Pound

An Encounter at St. Elizabeths
by Charles Olson

Edited by Catherine Seelye

Paragon House
NEW YORK

First Paperback edition, 1991

Published in the United States by

Paragon House
90 Fifth Avenue
New York, NY 10011

ACKNOWLEDGEMENTS

Grossman Publishers, The Estate of Charlies Olson, and Cape Goliard Press: From *Archaeologist of Morning* and *Maximus Poems* by Charles Olson, and from *Letters for Origin 1950–1956*, edited by Albert Glover.

New Directions Publishing Corporation: Edward Dahlberg, *Can These Bones Live*, Copyright 1941, © 1960 by Edward Dahlberg. D. G. Bridson, "An Interview with Ezra Pound" from *New Directions in Prose and Poetry #17*, Copyright © 1961 by New Directions Publishing Corporation, reprinted by permission.

New Directions Publishing Corporation and Faber and Faber Limited: Ezra Pound, *Pavannes and Divagations*, Copyright © 1958 by Ezra Pound. *Guide to Kulchur*, all rights reserved, Copyright © 1970 by Ezra Pound. *Personae*, Copyright 1926 by Ezra Pound. *Selected Prose 1909–1965*, all rights reserved, Copyright © 1973 by the Estate of Ezra Pound. Ezra Pound, *The Cantos*, Copyright 1934, 1937, 1948 by Ezra Pound, reprinted by permission.

Library of Congress Cataloging-in-Publication Data

Olson, Charles, 1910–1970.
    Charles Olson & Ezra Pound : an encounter at St. Elizabeths / by Charles Olson ; edited by Catherine Seelye. — 1st pbk. ed.
        p.   cm.
    Reprinted. Originally published: New York : Grossman Publishers, 1975.
    Includes bibliographical references.
    ISBN 1-55778-345-4
    1. Olson, Charles, 1910–1970—Friends and associates.   2. Pound, Ezra, 1885–1972—Friends and associates.   3. Poets, American—20th century—Biography.   4. Psychiatric hospital patients—United States—Biography.
    5. Saint Elizabeths Hospital (Washington, D.C.)—Biography.   I. Seelye, Catherine.   II. Title.   III. Title: Charles Olson and Ezra Pound.
    PS3531.082Z464   1991
    811'.52—dc20
    [B]   89-48875
                                                                        CIP

Manufactured in the United States of America

10 9 8 7 6 5 4 3 2 1

Fe, fi, fo, fum
I smell the joke of fas-cis-um
Be he victor or be he dead
I'll break his lie to make my bread

—Charles Olson

I am as deeply concerned about America as you are.

—Ezra Pound

When I told a friend I was undertaking the editing of Charles Olson's notes on Ezra Pound, the friend responded, "Oh dear, not another Pound book." I replied, "No, this will be an Olson book." And so it is.

When Olson died, he left behind a sizable collection of papers, included in which is a manila folder labeled "Pound case." Olson did not visit Pound with the intention of publishing his notes; it was not until much later in his life that he decided to do so, but he felt the project must await Pound's death. Olson was not to have this opportunity, for his own death preceded Pound's by two years. The University of Connecticut purchased Olson's library and papers, and this volume is one of several efforts to make public Olson's unpublished work.

The Pound file consists of two poems on Pound (and drafts thereof); several attempts in prose to reach an understanding of his feelings about the case (never entirely achieved); a few dozen pages of typed recollections of his meetings with Pound (some of which contain handwritten additions); a review of Ronald Duncan's *Journal of a Husbandman* (with Pound's critique); several pages of excerpts from *The Pisan Cantos*; a handful of correspondence from Pound, his wife, Dorothy, his son, Omar, his daughter, Mary de Rachewiltz, and others, pertaining for the most part to errands and social appointments, and containing many greetings to "Deah Chas" from "EP"; two small pocket notebooks in which Olson recorded bits of Pound's conversation, addresses, titles of books, and other such items; newspaper clippings relating to Pound's "capture" and upcoming trial; and so on. The more substantive of these papers are included in this volume. But running through Olson's journals of the period and through his published poetry are many comments concerning his relationship with and visits to Pound. I have incorporated a number of these in the Introduction.

Olson's prose style is not an easy one. He himself admitted that his style (here in reference to his poetry) is "damn irritating . . . (I do it gravely, as a part of, my method, believing that, resistance must be a part of style if, it is a part of the feeling)."[1]* The reader may take some solace from the fact that, for the most part, the chronicle here is in draft form and had not yet been hammered into "the proper sculpture."[2]

Among the irritations is the placement of punctuation, particularly commas. They remain as Olson used them. Another irritation is Olson's idiosyncratic use of parentheses, "opening, and then not closing a parenthesis, [which] is merely to acknowledge that just that way is the way one does parenthesize, actually: true to feeling (don't let the other convention trouble you, for it's only conventional)."[3] In a few cases, those where clarity and understanding of the notation seem to insist upon it, I have closed the parentheses.

All material, other than punctuation, added by me is enclosed in brackets. I have used no ellipses in the text—those that are used are Olson's. For omitted material I have said [words omitted]. Where handwriting was difficult to read, I have followed the questionable word with a [?]. Where handwriting was illegible I have said [illegible]. I have corrected spelling in a minimum of instances and never in proper names, names of books, and so forth. Material omitted was done so because of its probable offensiveness to living persons, and in no case was it germane to the issue here. The Appendix consists of selections from the notebooks (and backs of envelopes and other odds and ends of paper). I have omitted here

* Notes begin on page 115.

names and addresses; titles of books and other such routine nota-
tions; some material which appears in Olson's "Cantos"; some
often-quoted material which appears in Pound's *Cantos* (Adams on
Santayana's teaching at Harvard, Beardsley's "Beauty is difficult,"
and so forth); repetitious matter; and a few remarks by Pound on
his family.

All unpublished Olson material used and quoted throughout
for which no sources are given are in the Charles Olson Archives,
University of Connecticut Library. Olson's published poetry quoted
in the Introduction can be found in *Archaeologist of Morning* (New
York, 1970) or *The Maximus Poems* (New York, 1960). Quotations
from Olson's letters to Robert Creeley are from the Olson-Creeley
correspondence, presently being edited for publication by Donald
Allen and George Butterick. The two epigraphs are from unpublished
material in the Charles Olson Archives.

The annotations are rather numerous and fairly extensive, my
reason being that readers of Pound are not necessarily readers of
Olson and vice versa. My apologies to those who find too many
"obvious" notes and to those who may find an insufficiency.

Grateful acknowledgment of advice, patience, information, and
much of their time is made to George Butterick, Curator, Charles
Olson Archives; to Charles Boer, Literary Executor of the Charles
Olson Estate; to Jerome Kavka, Pound's doctor at St. Elizabeths;
and to the late Constance Wilcock Bunker, who knew the Olson of this
chronicle better than do any of us. My thanks go also to Donald
Allen for supplying a copy of an Olson letter and allowing me to
quote from it; to Mary Bowling for checking Pound's changes on
the proofs of Canto LXXIV, owned by Columbia University libraries;
to Malcolm Cowley for allowing the use of a letter from Olson to
him and to the Newberry Library for supplying a copy of the letter;
to Edward Dahlberg for allowing me to quote from a letter from
him to Olson and to John Cech for locating the quotation among
Dahlberg's letters; to C. David Heymann for searching the Federal

Bureau of Investigation's files on Pound for names of minor Italian government officials; to Frank Moore for spending an afternoon reminiscing about Olson and Washington and Pound; and to Mrs. William Carlos Williams for allowing me to print a letter from Williams to Olson. And for numerous helpful suggestions and information I am indebted to Charles Burkhart, Donald Gallup, Howard B. Gill, Hugh Kenner, James Laughlin, Harry Meacham, Noel Stock, Roger Stoddard, and Edward Weeks. Without the help of these people and others, this volume would be the poorer.

C.S.

Contents

Introduction

> *Olson saved my life.*[1]
> —Ezra Pound

The circumstances of Charles Olson's first meeting with Ezra Pound were hardly propitious. Pound, saved from a treason trial on grounds of insanity, had been locked away in St. Elizabeths Hospital in Washington, an isolation further enforced by the antagonism which his wartime broadcasts in Italy had aroused in former friends and fellow writers. For his own part, Olson was in a period of painful uncertainty, careers in teaching and politics behind him, his Black Mountain period ahead of him, and his major poetry yet to be written. The one man was bitter and old, nearing the sad end of a great career; the other was searching for some new means to an uncertain end. The result could hardly have been comparable to the master-disciple relationship of Pound and T. S. Eliot, and yet it was an important episode in the history of modern American poetry. The mark of Pound on Olson's work would probably be there even without the personal relationship, but it is Olson's artistic debt to Pound that underscores the importance of their meetings. For Olson came to pay his respects to Pound the poet, and his reverence for his work in the end conquered his aversion to the man Ezra Pound had become.

Olson visited Pound at St. Elizabeths over a period of two-and-one-half years. He was among the very first of Pound's visitors, having seen Pound for the first time on January 4, 1946, only two weeks after the finding that Pound was "insane and mentally unfit for trial." Olson's visit resulted from a suggestion by James Laughlin, Pound's friend and American publisher, to whom Olson had submitted "A Lustrum for You, E.P." Laughlin, in returning the manuscript, wrote, ". . . go around and see him . . . he can't seem to concentrate on reading or writing but he does enjoy talking to people —it seems to release some of his woes—and he's just as amusing to listen to as ever. You won't get a word in edgewise but you'll like it, I think." Olson did like it, in part. His visits during the first few months were almost weekly; their frequency thereafter diminished, partly owing to the increasing number of Pound's visitors and partly owing to Olson's disenchantment with Pound.

That Olson was very much interested in the Pound case months before his meeting Pound is shown by his defense of Pound, "This Is Yeats Speaking"; by his asking Dorothy Norman of *Twice-a-Year* to assign him the Pound trial; and by at least two poems, one sympathetic and the other savage, on the subject of Pound's postwar troubles. These two poems, along with the "Fragments," clearly reflect Olson's ambivalence concerning Pound, which never quite left him: on the one hand, an abhorrence of the "fascist and traitor," on the other, an enormous admiration for a great poet, and above all, a desire "to be of use if there was anything that could be done to save the scoundrel's skin," as he expressed it in a letter to Malcolm Cowley in April 1945.

Olson's more than casual interest in Pound is not surprising: he had listed his occupation as "writer" for years. As a writer, he was to observe in "GrandPa, GoodBye" that William Carlos Williams "was in Rutherford to be gone to, and seen, a clean animal, the only one we had on the ground, right here in the States." Now here was Pound to be gone to, and seen, perhaps not so clean, but in Washington, right under his nose. But in addition to Pound's allure as a writer, there was a second aspect which attracted (by repelling) Olson, the other side of "the tragic Double of our day": Pound the alleged fascist and traitor.

Olson's early judgments of Pound were often harsh, but his antipathy to Pound's political persuasions and his detestation of Pound's bigotry, seen at first hand early in the relationship, did not keep him away—not at first, that is. Olson's visits, at least the early ones, were the result of a combination of natural curiosity, a need to "prime the pump" (as he was shortly to admit to himself), and a very real compassion in the face of the suffering of a great poet. Olson's kindnesses were many, not the least of which was his providing some of the niceties of daily living lacking at St. Elizabeths. His visits in the face of the repulsion he often felt attest to his sincerity in his efforts to be of some comfort to Pound, the more so in view of his continuing disappointment over Pound's disinclination to discuss literature, particularly his own writing. Throughout it all, there was a strain of tenderness for and an understanding of Pound —indeed, even a great sympathy. He wrote of Pound in a notebook in 1947: "The sense of Pound's struggle to keep his head above things, against the others, Eliot, Joyce, Lewis, Yeats even." He wrote of himself in 1948: "the pathetic struggle to keep my own ego above their water." And it was this recognition in Pound of some of the same feelings of insecurity he was discovering in himself during this period that kept him returning month after month. For although Olson never loved Pound—unlike many others—he never hated him —unlike many others.

Pound's influence on Olson is well known and no doubt will occupy critics for years to come. How much Olson took from Pound (or Williams) is not of importance or the subject here—"God's spies" will have to determine the extent to which the "vermilion Guilt" appears on Olson's face.[2] It is sufficient to say that Olson was consciously aware of Pound as a model. A notebook entry for February 1945, for example, reads, "Maybe Pound discloses to you a method you spontaneously reached for. . . . Write as the fathers to be the father." And although a few years later he was to be tired of the Pound label, writing to Robert Creeley in 1951, "I am so sick of this biz of comparison 'like Pound,'" he saw in the label a criticism of Pound also and rose to defend him: "it is not those who know Pound that say this easy business of, like him, you, are like

him, but, those who still pipe for TSE [T. S. Eliot], always, it is
they—and the intent is, to beat me with that stick." Olson often
admitted that Pound was his master: "That the world had been
captured by Allen [Ginsberg] and Peter [Orlovsky] and Gregory
[Corso], and in fact their own master (like my Pound)."[3] And although he often turned from Pound, as in "I, Mencius, Pupil of the
Master. . ." ("We'll to these woods / no more, where we were used /
to get so much") and sometimes turned on him ("Look you old
bastard if you want open war come on [in] and get it"),[4] he never
forsook him entirely. In 1965, he was still "dragging my ass after
Ezra."[5] And in 1969 in answer to Gerard Malanga's question, "Does
Ezra Pound's teaching bear any relevance to how your poems are
formed on the page?" Olson responded, "My masters are pretty
pertinent. Don't cheat your own balloon."[6]

By the time Olson met Pound, he had been actively involved
in public life for several years. After a year as Chief of the Foreign
Language Information Service of the Common Council for American
Unity in New York, he went to Washington in 1942 as Assistant
Chief, Foreign Language Division, Office of War Information
(OWI), and in 1944 he became Foreign Nationalities Director
of the Democratic National Committee (DNC), a position which
put him third in command. His picture hung in Senator Claude
Pepper's office, and he was on a first name basis with several other
major political figures.

Olson left politics soon after the death of Roosevelt, whom he
revered, partly because he felt his destiny lay in writing but also
because he had little respect for many of the professional politicians
in the Democratic party. As Frank Moore put it,[7] the distance between the grandeur of politics under Roosevelt and the gutter politics
of Truman was too great for Olson. He simply could not bring
himself to work for "merchandise men / who get to be President."
Although Olson was active in politics only once again (the Presiden-

tial campaign of 1948), his political experiences were not alienating. That phase of his life was over—just that and no more.

But his experiences in Washington contributed significantly to the way in which he reacted to Pound. Olson's responsibility with the OWI was to get the war news out to Americans of foreign origin; his primary function with the DNC was to gather and deliver to the Democratic party the large foreign-nationality voting blocs. As the son of an immigrant father and a "first generation" mother, brought up in towns with large foreign populations (Worcester and Gloucester), Olson's own inherent sympathies and understanding of the problems encountered by ethnic groups were strengthened by his work in Washington. He wrote sometime during the war, "They call it 'the world war of survival'—and babel of 'American' lives as though American lives were somehow more precious than Russian, Filipino, Italian lives." He wrote in 1947, "If you must hate the Jew let us hate the Christian too." And in 1952, "my Portuguese"; and "my Nova Scotians, / Newfoundlanders, / Sicilianos, / Isolatos." Olson's identification of himself with minorities made impossible any lasting bond between Pound and himself. It was too big, too important to him, to ignore.

In some matters, however, Olson and Pound shared common views, although they frequently diverged in tone, emphasis, and intensity. While both lamented war, for example, with its tragic finale in death, Olson wrote, gently, in "Pacific Lament" of the death of "William Hickey, a member of the crew of the U.S.S. *Growler*, lost at sea in February, 1944." Pound wrote, bitterly, in *Hugh Selwyn Mauberley* of the deaths of "a myriad, / And of the best, among them, / For an old bitch gone in the teeth, / For a botched civilization." Although Olson worked for the war effort and was close to the center of power toward the end of the war, he still could write: "If we, the people, shall save ourselves from our leaders' shame, if we, the people, shall survive our disgust, if we, the people, shall end our own confusion, we must see this big war for the lie it is become. Make no mistake: it is a lie. Unwrap the charters and pacts. Recognize the deals. Stomach the people's hope for security. Tighten the soil over the men, always little men, who are dead. Call the big war what it is: a defeat for the people."

In spite of these feelings, Olson was a good American in the 1940s' sense of the words. Standing squarely in the center in 1944 he flailed both Left and Right. He said later of Lewis Frank, "I wouldn't speak to him for one year across a desk in Washington, sharing the same two secretaries, because I said to him, 'Until you acknowledge that you're a member of the Communist Party——.' "[8] At the same time, his outrage over the "libel, slander, rumor, lie, obscenity" by the fascist of "associations, classes, races, religions" spilled out in "People v. The Fascist, U.S. (1944)": "Attack is the first and final weapon of the fascist. Attack a leader, attack a class, attack a race—attack a peace. Always attack. . . . The fascists strike at 'Reds,' 'democrats,' 'Jews,' 'liberals,' 'Negroes,' 'Catholics.' "[9] In less than two years he was to meet Pound, author of "are you the arsenal of democracy or of judeocracy? And who rules your rulers? Where does public responsibility end, and what races can mix in America without ruin of the American stock, the American brain?"[10]

Olson was confronted head-on in these visits by the perennial problem of Pound's politics, unlike some who chose to ignore them, others who solved the problem by ignoring the man himself, and still others who believed, simply, that he was a "revolutionary simpleton." It is true, I think, that Pound's tragic flaw was his idealism (naïveté)—his belief, in this instance, that the good to be found in Fascism could be disassociated from the bad ("The Duce's aphorisms and perceptions can be studied apart from his means of getting them into action")[11] and that since he could make these distinctions all reasonable men could, and would. But Olson couldn't and wouldn't. He was appalled by Pound's fascism, whatever its brand, and reeled back from it time and time again only to find himself swept up time and again by Pound's disarming presence and charm.

Although Olson would have no truck with Pound's political views and raged against them (outside Pound's hearing), he listened more carefully to Pound's economic views, when they could be separated from the politics. His main complaint with Pound's economics at that time was Pound's old-fashioned strategy. Olson expressed it this way in a letter to Robert Creeley in 1951: "What I mean is, that, the 'politics' as was, then, the 30's (as of play to the Commies & all Neo-Revolutionists) was *good*, to be on, MONEY. And that MON is still of more moment than anyone but Ez and the bankers know. What has changed, is, that, it is [not] any longer of *use* to do the politicks as Ez then did it." Stamp scrip and national dividends appeared to Olson to be gimmickry, and he felt the nation's economic ills had gone beyond salvation by such methods. But if Olson did not agree with Pound's methods of economic reform, he did agree with many of the economic philosophies Pound was espousing. He had written before meeting Pound: "But the captains of industry ain't worth the powder etc. Take the Revolution so long as we're on the subject: whose revolution was it but the 'moneyed groups'; Breed's Hill two weeks after Lexington and it was all over for the 'smaller people' until Jefferson gave them another chance."[12] It is not surprising, therefore, that after meeting Pound a distinctly Douglasian[13] strain appears in Olson: "even when the money they [banks] are using for their usury is mine, solid, good earned money, for goods exchanged—my goods, obviously, being, when any money is earned, not the product of my labor but, the natural resources herein contained."[14]

When the subject came around to the connection between bankers and foreign policy, Olson seemed even more attentive. On the issue of war profiteering, Olson wrote to his friend Lewis Frank in 1946 about the possible need for a congressional investigation into the growth of monopolies during the war period and asked for data showing the relationship between banks and monopolies. Although there is no evidence that Olson pursued this matter, he did dispatch the idea of a *"Jewish* banking conspiracy"*: "They talk of Jews controlling the money of the country. But the 7 largest banking houses in the [country] are all Gentile, and the 8th, Kuhn, Loeb & Co. (partially Jewish) has but 2.88% of the international banking business; of 93,000 bankers & banking officials in the U.S. only 600 are Jews, and of 40 members of the governing committees of the N.Y. Stock Exchange only 3 are Jews."

Olson devoted a poem ("Issue, Mood," [1950]) to Pound's economics, ridiculing the naïve theories of Pound and the "funny-money boys." "O BOY, if that don't put / me *on!*" In the same year, however, he could write "To Gerhardt, there, among Europe's things . . ." in which he says, "The proposition, Gerhardt / is to get it straight, right / from the start. / Help raise the bones / of the great man." Yet it is apparent that Olson found it difficult to take his own advice, for he could never entirely get it straight about Pound: "the full shock of what a fascist s.o.b. Pound is"; "this man of exquisite senses"; "he is one/true/immediate/predecessor"; "these two inferior predecessors"; "he has such charm."

Still, on one point Olson never wavered: his deep-rooted aversion to Pound's views of class and race superiority: "Mr. Pound, I think, comes of a family which had means enough to take Ezra across the Atlantic. So he had the advantage of a European situation. I was born in south Worcester. That's a very important thing. I finally got pissed off at Ezra's pissing on Dr. Williams because one portion of Williams was Jewish—about 1/16, 1/18, 1/9, 1/8, 1/4, 1/7, 1/17. . . ."[15]

Throughout his visits, Olson was hard put at times to sit quietly in the face of Pound's diatribes. That he managed to do so results partly from a genuine desire to avoid embarrassment for both Pound and himself and partly from his self-deprecating habit, which he deplored, of becoming silent in the presence of greater figures ("men who have more work behind them"). However little he said to Pound, with himself he was voluble on the subject of this relationship which was giving him so many personal and philosophical problems.

Olson was thirty-five years old when he met Pound. He was yet to publish his first major work (his published literary *oeuvre* at this point consisted of two articles and four occasional poems). He had abandoned first the academy and then politics to write his book on Melville. And when it was written, he was cast loose. A mammoth without direction. He was floundering and knew it. He had observed in "The K" in 1945 that "there is a tide in a man / moves him to his moon and, / though it drop him back / he works through ebb to mount / the run again and swell / to be tumescent I." Olson was at his lowest ebb during the period of his visits to Pound, a "failure in my work and life." In search of the "tumescent I," he railed against himself, writing in his notebook in 1947: "The job, given the obvious I am a writer, to be as decisive, careless, productive, & direct as I was as politician! How to do that! There it is, brother."

During this period he dug and probed into himself, and his notebooks record that he discovered many things: "What you are is what you took from others. As new tree reaches out of compost." The others were "Finch, Melville, Dahlberg, Cagli, & even Pound."[16] Olson eventually rejected his surrogate fathers, writing to Creeley in 1951, for example, that "(Melville, for me, now likewise) is *backward*, and distasteful." That he recognized his need for one father after another and that they were ultimately harmful to him is apparent from a notebook entry in 1948, shortly before his break with Pound.

> the mark [of] my resistance at any longer being a son. For it is a mere son I have been till now. (the way I have leaned on each of men mentioned for direction of work, decisions, gone to them to prime the pump. In each case,

however, the love has been covert, & the work posed as my own. The price I have paid is the *resistance* to them, which has racked me—the pathetic struggle to keep my own ego above their water. . . .

the character of the resistance is this: I would rather be less than I dream myself to be & to be myself than any longer strive to be something each of these men could admire. It's entirely possible I may have to fall way back behind what I might think (or they) I am capable of, in order to find my own proper base. I have this feeling: that I can only come to have any feeling & directness by so doing. . . .

Cagli & Pound are obviously my present unresolved "amours."

Olson was determined to rid himself of his feelings of inadequacy in the presence of greater men and he recognized that to do so meant ridding himself of the men themselves. Thus, the Pound "amour" did not stay long unresolved. "I got myself called a Semite by telling Ezra Pound that my grandmother's name was Lybeck, which is obviously Lubeck."[17] Olson told Robert Creeley that this was "a trap on purpose laid to make the taker mad." Why? First, he was tired of the visits. It was easy to become tired of Pound. One of Pound's psychiatrists remarked that "one didn't have a mutual dialogue with him—he was at you."[18] And e.e. cummings said that "in everyone's relations with Mr. Pound there come . . . coolnesses."[19] Also, he was sick of Pound's anti-Semitism. But perhaps the overriding reason lies in Olson's old problem with fathers, a truth he was willing to admit at that time only to himself.[20]

The break was complete except for a few last sporadic sputterings of correspondence. There was communication of a kind in 1951 between Olson and Pound through John Kasper, who was interested in publishing a "selected Olson" and in getting Olson involved in the Square Dollar Series.[21] Creeley, wary of Kasper and warning

Olson to be careful in his dealings with him, suggested that Kasper might be Pound's attempt at a reconciliation. Olson wrote back: "can't figure it, any more than you do, how come they are ready to run me in there, as 2nd horse in the race for the Square Dollar Purse, with the Big Red! Damn well wish that might have happened!"

Olson did not see Pound again until 1965, at the eighth annual Festival of Two Worlds in Spoleto. Seeing Pound again "was like having an Umbrian angel suddenly descend upon you. . . . It was very beautiful the way the fierceness of Pound had settled down into a voiceless thing which only responded twice to me."[22] Olson had written "The Song of Ullikummi," which "I read, unhappily I guess, because nobody else said a word, in front of Ezra Pound . . . in honor of him. . . . I read it as a translation, trying to honor the fact that I thought Mr. Pound really, justly, freed the languages of the world." But "it fell dead."[23] They were not to meet again.

Were this chronicle simply a record of Pound's first years at St. Elizabeths it would be of no particular importance. There would seem to be little call for dragging out for public scrutiny a great poet's rather seamy side, for the picture of Pound which Olson presents is just that. It is for the most part the familiar Pound on Jews, Pound on economics, Pound on publishers, Pound on his enemies (and friends). The poet is rarely seen. Nor is there much evidence of the bubbling exuberance, the magical language, the delightful arrogance which so enchanted his admirers in earlier days. There are, instead, sad glimpses now and then of a confused, depressed, and exhausted man, living to a large extent in the past. While it is apparent at times that the "early" Pound still existed, Olson, at home following a visit, full of bottled up rage and shock, poured out his reactions with little effort to present an undistorted picture.

The picture of himself, however, that Olson presents here is a rare one. Although he was surfacing as a literary figure (*Call Me Ishmael*, his first major work, was published in March 1947), he was not well known during this period outside the small circles of Melville scholars and Washington political figures. Therefore, the record of Olson's encounter with Pound is valuable as it enlightens us concerning this critical period in Olson's life. We have here the master and the pupil together, the one a great poet who has reached the zenith of his literary career, the other a little known poet just beginning his, the one an alleged Fascist-sympathizer, the other a New Deal Democrat, the one a "Continental" American, the other one generation removed from the "Continent." And if Olson, as has been argued by many, is an important figure in modern poetry, if indeed he is a pivotal figure, the clarion of the changing of the guard, this, then, is a significant meeting and a necessary part of the record.

Though there is very little to be found in this record of Pound's literary influence on Olson, there is reason to believe that his visits with Pound figured in the transformation of Olson from a minor prose writer to a poet writing in the tradition of Pound and Williams. For in Olson's notebooks of the period, we see him almost frantically searching for an identity, for an impulse, for a focus, for a framework strong enough to support his "special view of history." And in Olson's "Cantos" on Pound, we see him during this same period face to face with perhaps the most potent literary influence of his life. Out of these forces came *Maximus*, Olson's "tumescent I." Somewhere "among the ruins," Charles Olson found his poetic voice.

But Olson's chronicle is more important as a record of a personal and political encounter, the confrontation of a man of good conscience and a man of hate—the issue of politics as opposed to poetry, which is the central issue of Ezra Pound. An issue which many were (and are) loathe to face. And Olson, whatever his reasons, faced it head-on. For although he came to see the poet, he stayed to help the man.

C.S.

A Lustrum
for You, E.P.

1
So, Pound, you have found the gallows tree
you with your thumb at your nose
the word in your mouth dirty, and otherwise.

They'll cant your body, canto maker.
Sudden, and your freckled neck will break
as others', nameless, broke.

There was Booth's collaborators in a gray Washington snow
after another war.
Matthew Brady's camera slanted, one by one, to each adjustment
                                        of the noose.
Or do they shoot you now

2
You wanted to be historic, Yorick.
Mug the mike with your ABCs
you even made Sligo Willie sneeze:
revolutionary simpleton.
Ezra Pound, American.

Sing out, sing hate.
There is a wind, mister
where the smell, o anti-semite

3

in the nose is as
vomit, poet.

I quote: in a modern city the live man feels
or perceives this sort of thing as the savage
perceives in the forest.

3
You are your own best witness.
These are not the great days.
No hunt, sir, and what you take for bays,
Propertius, are the rattle of cans.

4
Listen, Montana, you've been right about a lot, sure.
The Civil War did drive everything out of the American mind,
you and Martin Van Buren included.
You have also said, a propos Jefferson and/or Pound: the
real life in regular verse is an irregular movement UNDERNEATH.

Private gain is not prosperity, but that the treasure of
a nation is its equity?

Yes, if a man isn't willing to take some risk for his
opinion, either his opinions are no good or he's no good.
Remember Heine? You have admired him. He walked through
a revolution too. He didn't have his eyes left, and he
wasn't as gay as you. It was paresis laid him low. (What
got you?) He left what he called his mattress grave and
found his way, blind, through the bullets in the street,
it was 1848, to the Louvre. He did it, he took the risk,
to have another look at Venus. What did you go to see
in a broadcasting studio?

5
There is a court
where order, traitor
—you stood with the lovers of ORDER
 19 years on that case/first case
keeps the fragrance of,
sometimes in the palm of a hand
also on street corners,
hyacinth and burnt feathers

Where the wind is a warm breath
it does not smell of flesh in a furnace

6
The sentence reads: lover of the obscene
      by the obscene undone

    fecit, Pound fecit

Your Witness

name Pound, Ezra   born Montana   1887

journalist. As I see it history of today
literature is that stays news

. . a poem here and there. The live man
in a modern city feels this sort of thing or
perceives it as the savage perceives in the forest

I guess so yes if you mean a crank is
any man ANY other ambition save that of
saving his own skin from the tanners

I think the American system *de jure*
Adams Jefferson VAN BUREN
is probably quite good enough if
only 500 men (save that) with guts
the sense to USE it
or even with the capacity for
answering letters or
printing a paper

. . one should respect intelligence

. . another war without glory, another peace without quiet

9

The real life in regular verse is an irregular
movement underneath. Jefferson
thought the formal features of the American system
would work, and they did work till the time of Grant
but the condition of their working was that there
should be a *de facto* government composed
of sincere men willing the national good

. . the centre holds by attraction

I offer the hypothesis that: When a single mind
sufficiently ahead of the mass a one-party
system is bound to *occur as actuality* whatever
the details of form in administration

The CIVIL WAR drove everything out of the American mind.
Perhaps the worst bit of damage was it drove out
of mind the first serious anti-slavery candidate
not because he was an anti-slavery candidate but
because he saved the nation and freed the American
treasury

Well, if I ain't worth more alive than dead, that's that

. . that private gain is not prosperity, but that
the treasure of a nation is its equity

If a man isn't willing to take some risk for his opinion,
either his opinions are no good or he's no good

A good government is one that operates according to the best
that is known and thought. And the best

government is that which translates the best
thought most speedily into action

19 years on this case/first case. I have set down part of

. . stand with the lovers of

ORDER

Fragments

1945

I can't figure it out—how the questions raised by the Pound case have gone unexamined, [illegible], unquestioned. I can't understand how men who have owed so much have continued in silence. I am not thinking of protest. I am not talking about any consideration of

I am not talking about

I hate this anti-semite! this revolutionary simpleton, as Yeats called him. Go further and wonder, as Yeats did, if his Cantos aren't all hodos chameliontos.[1] But for christ's sake have the courage to admit that Pound faced up to the questions of our time. I think he shows himself a traitor to more important things than the U.S. No man can attack a race and remain useful to anyone as an artist. But let any man beware who is a party to a state condemnation of a man. Let him beware more for himself than for Pound if he has not examined the premises of justice as we know it. Let him remember that justice is on trial itself today.

15

It is not enough to call him a fascist.

He is a fascist, the worst kind, the intellectual fascist, this filthy apologist and mouther of slogans which serve men of power. It was a shame upon all writers when this man of words, this succubus, sold his voice to the enemies of the people.

I cannot be responsible for the way the Dept. of Justice tries the citizen Ezra Pound. But I say I nor any other writer can allow Ezra Pound the writer to go untried. For he stands forth in all his violence to be judged. It is here the fact that he is a poet, and a good one, has bearing. It is not, as I hear it said, in relation to his trial by the state. These are not times like Milton's to recall Pindar and plead exception for a writer. Because he is a writer, this case of Ezra Pound deserves to be examined by the men who share his responsibility:

I propose that what has not been done since his indictment be now done because his public trial is a trial of all of us who use the word. This man, who is as good as any of us, is a fascist. We will get further if we include treason in the larger conspiracy. For treason is not necessarily a crime within the world of creation.

It is against such background only that Ezra Pound can be properly tried and I propose that he be so examined and tried by the only men who conceivably can recognize and judge him, his fellow writers. It is not as traitor to the U.S., but as fascist he should be judged. It is not his radio broadcasts, but the whole body of his work that should be the testimony.

16

Such a trial is long overdue. It cannot, now that he shall be publicly tried, any longer be postponed. For it is already clear that though he shall be tried in court as Jane Anderson & Kaltenbach,[2] as a mere hired hand of a foreign government with whom we were at war, we shall find that the press and the people will try him as the Poet Ezra Pound.

This is where his craft comes in. You and I know Pound is not crazy, one of those "poets." You and I know he is as gifted and trained and skillful a poet as any man who has written the English language in these years of our century. We may find him exterior. But there is none but the small who will deny him his power. Read only "The Return." If you will thus turn aside, go and be damned, your tongue will never fork with fire. You do not have a ghost.

Try this man, writer, and then condemn him. Shall the State do what men, whose business it is to come by truth, do not do? Shall we talk a 100 Cantos and not answer the anti-semite who wrote them? Shall we learn from his line and not answer his lie? For let us be clear about this. I hear it said: a poet must be tried to prove that poets are responsible citizens. This is a cropper, easy to see. You as I know a writer's responsibility *as writer* is to his own sense of life, without regard to state, to system, to idea or to justice. Pound himself, when he was picked up, put it this way: "If a man hasn't the guts to gamble his opinion, then his opinion isn't worth anything or he himself." Let us, then, in the world of our value, separate from the state, examine the work of Pound. He would be the first to stake his work as social in consequence. He is no poet to separate his poetry from society. He is a writer of purpose: I remember a remark of his in his ABC of Economics, something about the proposition of our time and the central theme of all creation to lie not in the Hamlet question, to be, but to eat, or not to eat.[3]

Can any man, equipped to judge, find Pound other than a serious man? Can any writer honestly argue with those who shall, do call him a crank? It's no good, that business. Around his trial you will hear it again and again. Just one of those goddamned writers. They're crazy. A Bohemian. There are writers who are such, but not Pound, despite all the vomit of his conclusions.

Two trials: a nationalist, or a Big three trial is, in the nature of the war they follow, empty of meaning. For the premise of civil war, international civil war, has long since been given up. Only an admission of it gives a frame in which Hess[4] or Ezra Pound can be judged.

It is no surprise that this frame is absent from the Trials. It is a surprise that the case of Ezra Pound has not been examined out of court in this frame of reference. It gives cause for despair that no magazine in England or America or France has, to my knowledge, "tried" Pound in the full light of his career. It was obvious from the start that his state trial would be based on his broadcasts, and that he would be judged within these limits as Jane Anderson and Kaltenbach will be judged with him. Let that be: it is so, and so it shall be.

But that Pound should, by those who have learned from him, be allowed to remain ignored as a Jane Anderson and a Kaltenbach is another matter. For Pound is no dried whore of fascism. He is as brilliant a maker of language as we have had in our time. The point is not that this mitigates, or in any way relates to the punishment the U.S. shall deal to him as an American citizen. What is called for is a consideration, based on his career, of how such a man came to the position he reached when he allowed himself to become the voice of Fascism. For Pound is not isolated in this, among artists of his time. He is only, as so often, the more extreme. Yeats, Lewis, Lawrence have also been labeled fascist.

The Pound case is the base from which one of the most important crises of our time can, for the writer, painter & musician, be most satisfactorily examined. For behind his art lies a respect for authority & behind that respect lies a disrespect for democracy as we are acquainted with it. It is time we examined censury, without patriotism, admitting such evil as anti-semitism——

Fascism captured criticism of democracy, & puts any critic in the camp of the enemy. It is time we faced this. For the danger is what happened to a Pound. From this point of view he was driven

The point for examination is the point at which authority shifts to the authoritarians.

Respect for authority as it is tradition & authority as it is state system.

We have reached a situation in which several of our chief writers, in revolt against the cult of the common man, have come dangerously close to alliance with the cult of the elite. Pound went all the way over.

If he were not first rate, it would be of little interest, mere sociology. If it were Auden and not Yeats, it would be the same. If it were his imitators and not D. H. Lawrence, so. But these three men, and James Joyce, constitute the major forces in the generation out of which we who are young now come. Is it not significant that all three should have gone so far away from

Pound is an exterior man. His work, too. And all his culture was so much stuff in a hole to keep the wind away.

The Trial of Ezra Pound

So Pound is tried for treason. Pound broadcast, the State speaks back. His penny postcards, cancelled Rapallo, addressed Rutherford, N.J., come home to roost.

The U.S. v. E.P. is a consequence, a game. It has its drama. The press smells it, is on the scent: the Poet Ezra Pound. . . . The trial will give a flush of satisfaction to Pound's enemies. Perhaps to Pound: it is a climax to a side of him. Suddenly he is in history, along with John Adams and Martin Van Buren. He is elected by indictment. Briefly, negatively, the push to politics, always in him Montana on, the pulsator of the Cantos, that American poem, erupts him into a part in a play of power.

He enters—at exit. Of a drama he is, at last, *persona*. A rope could redden his freckled neck.

Consequence. It's the fun of the game. Truth's a bore. It won't be present at the trial. The Pound trial, like the trial of Goering and Streicher,[5] is already emptied of meaning. The frame's askew. The only premise by which any of them could be brought to proper justice is lacking. It was lacking in the war just fought.

There was a time not long ago when these wars of our days were understood to be international civil war. They were seen to be a part of a struggle I find more point now than ever in calling the new Hundred Years War. Date it from 1905.

We shall not try this Pound, this Streicher. We have not moved out, as some men who died in Spain, far enough. Pound, Streicher,

21

Goering are not enemies of one state, instruments of nations, Germany, Italy, only. They will come closer to trying us, for they have gained, in their conspiracy, a critical vantage. They are already international, as we are unprepared to be. We have not yet shaped, because we have denied this civil war, a justice with sanctions strong and deep enough to measure the crime.

[We have] a peculiar lack of interest in the fate of Ezra Pound. I find the silence lame and pitiful. I think of Yeats, who was a father too, and ask myself if he would have let these events go by without examination. I wonder why T. S. Eliot, William Carlos Williams, Wyndham Lewis, other men who have known Pound all these years have not told us how they explain him. They knew him better than we younger men.

I am fed up with the easy

Thoughts on Yeats
Ideas on Ezra Pound

So Pound is tried for treason. Pound broadcast, the State speaks back. His penny postcards come home to roost. The trial is consequence and though the drama may please Pound and satisfy his enemies, the momentous thing lies back a piece in time. Not is he traitor, but when and how come did his sense of authority, a poet's possession, slip off and become identified with the Authoritarian State?

This calls for examination, because other men wrestle on this ground. There was a time, a few years ago, when these wars of our days were understood to be international civil war. The recent phase of battle against fascist nations has obscured the issue of this new Hundred Years War. Thus these trials, of Goering and Streicher, as of Pound, are emptied of meaning. These men are not indicted, any more than the war was fought, in reference to world civil war. Justice is still the rambling railer we are familiar with. The enemy is Germany, Italy, and these international conspirators are brought to an old justice. The new justice stays where the new world keeps itself alive, in the chaos which moves irresistibly ahead in the mass of the billions of the earth's peoples who have not yet taken their head.

What constitutes "our" side is not easy to see or state: to go no further than the term "democracy," left or center, it is too lazy, too dead of the past to include the gains of the present and advances

23

to come. But the enemy, because he attacks, stands clear. A "fascist" is still a definition.

We shall not try this Pound, this Streicher. We have not moved out, as some men who died in Spain, far enough. These men are not enemies of the state, traitors, instruments of nations, Germany, Italy, alone. They will come closer to trying us, for they have gained, in their conspiracy, a critical vantage. They are already international, as we are unprepared to be. We have not yet shaped, because we have denied this civil war, a justice with sanctions strong and deep enough to measure the crime. Our own case remains unexamined. How then shall we try men who have examined us more than we have ourselves? They know what they fight against. We do not yet know what we fight for.

It does not surprise me that Ezra Pound will not be tried.

This Is Yeats Speaking

1945

This is William Butler Yeats. I want to speak to my friends in America about a thing which troubles me even now, though I have recovered leisure, and know more than I did about structure, mathematical and otherwise.

It is my friend Ezra Pound—who has made so many beautiful things. You Americans, you have him now on trial. I remember I warned him once about politics, not as you think, that we poets should stay out of it, I said simply, do not be elected to the Senate of your country. I was thinking of my own experience. I merely observed, you and I are as much out of place as would be the first composers of Sea-shanties in a age of Steam.

I am not very interested in your hysteria, or his. We of Ireland have lived with treason long. It is not as dramatic as Ezra thinks, he has always been in these things as in so much American, exterior, moral. When he shouted, and now I hear you shout, I stoop down and write with my finger on the ground.

I do not know that any of us of my generation, and few of yours —I too a revolutionist—understand the contraries which are now engaged. William Blake observed that oppositions do not make true contraries.

It was our glory, Pound's and mine, I except Eliot—tradition is too organized with him, his uncertainty before chaos leads him to confuse authority with orthodoxy—to reassert the claims of authority in a world of whiggery. It is true what Pound said, we men of the mind do stand with the lovers of order. We value it, with what labor

27

we purchase it in our work. We opposed ourselves to a leveling, rancorous, rational time.

What a man of Eliot's words would call our sin was the opposite of his. Willing as we were to oppose and go forward, we did not seek true contrary. Because of your irascible mind, Pound, and because my bones always took to comfort like a retainer's, you were ever in haste, and I sometimes, to think these men who marched and preached a new order—we of our excitable profession are attracted to sick men and buccaneers—had taken that other chaos of men's lives up in their hands, had worked to master it as we do ours, and could shape what men now need, rest, an end to this sea of question.

I understand this, at the distance I have acquired, I have Troilus' vantage, from the seventh sphere to look back on Diomed and Cressid both.

It was Pound's error to think, because he was capable to examine with courage and criticize eloquently the world we have inherited —Rapallo was a place to escape the knots of passion, it was the village in the Chinese poem to which the official retire, inhabited by old men devoted to the classics—Pound thought this power, necessary to us men who had to make the language new, also gave him the sight to know the cure. It is the frenzy that follows when the mask of a man is askew. The being must brag of its triumph over its own incoherence.

I examine his work in this new light and when he lay with beauty in her corner or fed cats in the street, they have their oppressors, he was a true lover of order. I would undo no single word or all he has published, quarrel as I have with him, take as I did at times his work of twenty years, the Cantos, to be a botch of tone and colour, all Hodos Chameliontos.

He was false—out of phase—when he subordinated his critical intelligence to the objects of authority in others. If the Positive Man do that, all the cruelty and narrowness of his intellect are displayed in service of preposterous purpose after purpose till there is nothing left but the fixed idea and some hysterical hatred.

It was natural he looked for an elite, and from brawlers and poets. It was his obsession to draw all things up into the pattern of art. He was ignorant of science and he will be surprised, as Goethe will not be, to find a physicist come on as Stage Manager of the tragedy.

It is a time, yours, when forces large as centuries battle and I suppose you must be more violent in your judgment than a man like me who had age tied to his tail like a can. But this I would say to you: you must take strength by embracing the criticism of your enemy. It is the beauty of demons they rush into struggle with a cry of hate you must hear if you will answer them.

I have advanced far enough out of the prison of my generation to understand it is civil war in which you are locked.

> What day you ask when date is dead
> of May, when month is lost.
> I can be precise though it is no answer:
> this is the day of great year
> the day of fear.
> Man is moon.

You will know better than I know how it is to be fought. I wrote to my wife one time from Rapallo when I had listened to Pound for an afternoon damn usury, expound credit and Major Douglas, talk the totalitarian way, it was as though I were in the presence of one of Wyndham Lewis' revolutionary simpletons.

I had never read Hegel, but my mind had been full of Blake from boyhood up, I saw the world as a conflict, and could distinguish between a contrary and a negation. Yet it was not easy for me to listen when one of your young men who had come to Rapallo to see Pound came away and said to me: "He has mingled with ferret and Chameleon, vulture and kite, every anti-semite after his kind. He has touched abomination and is unclean." (Do I understand, now that I am more familiar with the Old Testament world?)

CHARLES OLSON & EZRA POUND

In my first hard spring-time I had a friend I thought half a lunatic, half knave.

> And I told him so, but friendship never ends;
> And what if mind seem changed,
> And it seem changed with the mind,
> When thoughts rise up unbid
> On generous things that he did
> And I grow half contented to be blind![1]

Now in your country I hear a department called Justice speak of scripts for wireless and Ezra, as I would expect, talk back sharp. (Words cause no man fear except in the making of them.) I pay little heed, though there is pity in me, for I know Pound, he is a gambler and can measure consequence.

The soul is stunned in me, o writers, readers, fighters, fearers, for another reason, that you have allowed this to happen without a trial of your own. It is the passivity of you young men before Pound's work as a whole, not scripts alone, you who have taken from him, Joyce, Eliot and myself the advances we made for you. There is a court you leave silent—history present, the issue the larger concerns of authority than a state, Heraclitus and Marx called, perhaps some consideration of descents and metamorphoses, form and the elimination of intellect.

We were the forerunners—Pound only the more extreme—but our time was out of phase and made us enders. Lawrence among us alone had the true mask, he lacked the critical intelligence, and was prospective. You are the antithetical men, and your time is forward, the conflict is more declared, it is you to hold the mirror up to authority, behind our respect for which lay a disrespect for democracy as we were acquainted with it. A slogan will not suffice.

It is a simple thing I ask as I might question a beggar who stopped me for a coin. It is the use, the use you make of us.

Are you a court to accept and/or reject JEFFERSON AND/OR

MUSSOLINI, indict GUIDE TO CULTURE and write a better, brief me contrary ABCs, charge why 100 CANTOS betrays your country, that poem which concerns itself so much with the men who made your Revolution for you? I have said I often found there brightly printed kings, queens, knaves but have never discovered why all the suits could not be dealt out in some quite different order. What do you find, a traitor?

Dean Swift says in a meditation on a woman who paints a dying face,

> Matter as wise logicians say
> Cannot without a form subsist;
> And form, say I as well as they,
> Must fail, if matter brings no grist.

What have you to help you hold in a single thought reality and justice?

Cantos

1946–1948

First Canto, January 5, 1946

I met Pound for the first time yesterday. I had seen him once before, on November 27, at his arraignment before Bolitha Laws,[1] when he stood mute. That day his eyes crossed mine once, and they were full of pain, and hostile, cornered as he was in a court, with no one he knew around him except his lawyer[2] whom he had only known a week. The moment when he, a man of such words, stood up mute before the court, had its drama, personal. But earlier, before Laws entered, there was another moment, a political one. Pound's lawyer called his attention to a jury waiting in the box for some rooming house trial which was to follow Pound's arraignment on Laws' calendar that morning. It was a typical jury, that collection of free men which constitutes that right of the democratic process, TRIAL BY JURY, easy to satirize, common as it is, to burlesque, unliterate as the people are, to caricature, lumpish as they appear in public place. There it was, and Pound swung round in his chair to confront it. For forty years of exile he had turned his tongue against America, for twenty years he had damned democracy and its works. Now, at bay, his own life soon would be in the hands of some suchagathering of twelve men. He hunched forward, shot his head up and out like a beak, and squinting his eyes as though he missed glasses, though he had them on, moved along the jurors faces, squaring at each direct and dwelling, as children and poets will and nobody else does because it is supposed to be rude. His face told nothing, his eyes were as they were towards me, and I would guess

35

he was too distracted by his own troubles for his feelings to come to bear on this thing before him. The courtroom remained in its state of piety and quiet. This was the chief justice's chambers, made like some Episcopal chapel, with Negroes filling the pews for wit-nesses, and on the other side of the bench, raised up like an altar, opposite the jurors' box, lawyers and the press and attendants talked low. Nothing disturbed the piety and quiet. It was a sleepy, do nothing world, waiting. What was in the moment lay outside it, stretching back a long way, with Pound's sixty years from Idaho on measured against those several hundred years since some Englishmen first filed in and made a jury. Pound finished his examination and turned away to more immediate things, fingering one wrist with the other hand, removing his glasses and rubbing his eyes, slumping in his chair and then leaning on the table, twisting for comfort, always working his hands.

He was so alone that day, and worn down, I wanted to put out my hand and say some friendly thing. I had never seen him before and took him to look older and weaker than I had imagined. His veins were starting out on his temples, his wrists looked thin and his hands too long. His stance at the elevator, going out. And his refusal of the N.Y. Times.[3] He was grey and alone. That is why yesterday I was surprised. For his hand was as strong or more than my own. And his flesh was fresh and strong.

His eyes were no longer hooded with hate. His eagerness and vigor as he came swiftly forward into the waiting room. The open-ness in his eyes. And shyness at looking too long at me, turning away, toward window. Still working at his forehead with his thumb, index and middle finger, occasionally as he did so much in court. I marked his emotion most when he spoke of Mary and Omar,[4] his loneliness and worry about them, as he looked out the window, and his eyes seemed inside his stomach. And I told him he looked better than when I saw him last. When was that? Nov 27. O, don't mention dates, I can't remember them. Was it when I talked in the court. No, when you stood mute. It was Gallinger,[5] I rested there. You see they took me from Pisa to Rome in a jeep, gave me only half an hour . . . "I don't know how much you know about all this." I answered: "Some of it." And he went on . . . the plane avoided Frankfurt, apparently because of the overcast, we stopped at the Azores, but then on to here.[6] The jail at first was all right (gesturing to a high ceiling) and I wasn't bothered by claustrophobia. But then that break, and they put us in cells.

Gallinger was better than this (indicating with head and eyes Howard Hall, at St Elizabeths, its high penitentiary wall outside the barred window). All these padlocks and doors. (The building goes back to the 80s and 90s, and I had been let in through a black iron door with nine peep holes cut in it in 3 horizontal rows.) There's an Indian in my ward who talks all the time about killing people. Last night he got the number up to 10,000 he wanted to bump off. (The same use of outdated slang as in his work.)

I think it was then Pound for the first time mentioned his things at Gallinger, papers, clothes, money to get the boy to go for papers and candy bars for him. He kept coming back to it. He feels lost without them, naturally, wants some personal things to occupy him. Suggested I write cards to people asking him to write to him, and explain he could not answer. He can't seem to put down more than one or two sentences. I made as to do it, but he said, my addresses are at Gallinger. We will have to wait. Zeiman told me later, or was it Kavka,[7] he would like to hear from his old friends—Cummings, Z[ukofsky] mentioned. I thought of Bill Williams.

Then told me how at Pisa he had written the *Cantos* (turned out to be ten) and done the *Confucius*.[8] He said he owed that to a Jew in Rome[9] (or was it Chew?[10] I couldn't be sure, and did not want, at this first meeting, to interrupt him).

He was most gracious about his talking, though. Explained one gets egotistical in a place like this! Made an effort to allow me to also speak. Was neat about who I was. Is it possible I have seen your name on something in print?

The proofs of the *Confucius* he thought would be no trouble but the *Cantos*, though he did not mention them, appeared to be another matter, on his mind. Here as elsewhere he indicated Laughlin vaguely, apparently on the assumption I was from him and knew about these things.

He wanted something to do. He complained of treating a man for dyptheria when he had dysentery. He said, quite quietly, he didn't think there was anything wrong with him. Admitted his mind was distracted and said if he had to stay there much longer he would go bust. Kept using some word like souvenirs, or splinters, which conveyed to me the opposite sense of what he meant. I took it to be good, and he meant it would be the bad outcome if he did bust. Wanted to leave something before he went—"for his family."

Talked quite rapidly about Mary, something of Omar having gone to Rome, and then about their arriving in Rapallo on May 20, when he had expected them on the 17th. And he was taken away the night of the 16. Apropos of this he mentioned his clothes, and explained when the partigianos came to the door with their tommy-guns he had put on what he had worn since, because he didn't know what kind of floors of what Italian jails he'd be lying on.

At one point, as of Howard Hall,[11] showed the strength of curiosity inherent in any creative man, when he said even Gorilla Cage[12] was something for awhile! Always referred to it as Gorilla Cage. Spoke of how good they treated him at CIC.[13] And remembered his tent at Pisa as endurable. They did not know, he said, when they started him off for the U.S., that he had only been on his feet in the tent about two hours a day. They couldn't see.

What's behind it all, who wants this thing? For a moment I didn't gather he meant that somebody seemed to want these things to happen to him. "Who is this Truman? Does his name happen to be

Warren Gamaliel?"[14] To which I replied, you will have to take his name as it sounds and judge the lie from that. (This might sound like persecution, but in the light of the Army's Cage for him and a few other things, hasn't he a right to wonder?)

He made a point they didn't know about his work inside Italy. It appeared he was suggesting he had worked with the liberals on the inside against Mussolini. He mentioned ———, the head of Propaganda,[15] and said he was liberal, and had told him he couldn't walk on the side of the street under M's Palazzo because of the stink of the boss! Other things I have forgotten.

At another time declared, would they rather listen to Klaus Mann[16] than me? This surprised me, and I said, when he was a young man it must have been the same, lessers were preferred. Put my hand out and touched his arm above the wrist as it lay on the table and remarked, the old Yankee preachers (thinking of his own forefathers) used to call it innate depravity. And told him how I had met Klaus Mann at Laughlin's party for Bill Williams and K had mistaken me for L. I said, he was looking for him. And P retorted, He would be looking for a publisher!

At the time he mentioned his inside work in Italy he pulled on me the same thing he had on the press his first day here, the idea of going to Tiflis to learn Georgian so that he could be sent to talk to Stalin. Emphasized how little attention Stalin would pay to some fat from the State Department talking the old bankers line. Said so far as he knew they had one man in the State Dept who spoke Georgian.

And when he asked who Truman was, he swung off on how he had lacked recent information. No *Congressional Directory* later than I think 1939. And then a list of what he had based his work on, especially Brooks Adams. And challenged if Adams was a Fascist. Repeated it. From which I backed away. For I do not want to engage in politics with him. I have declared myself on that, felt my way through, and come to a judgment. I don't wish to get into it. I dare say I will have to, and probably the best thing is to leave him my Yeats speaking, if it comes up. I wish only to offer him some personal comforts, do some chores for him like getting people to write to him, and give him an ear more or less able to be sympathetic. And this, for the work he has done. And what I now feel, the charm and attraction of his person. For he is as handsome and quick and at work as ever. His jumps in conversation are no more than I or any active mind would make. Once in awhile he seems to speak with an obsession, but even this I do, and at his age, after the fullness of his life, I imagine I might be a hell of a lot worse. I think of Dahlberg already.

He unloaded on the English. Stated radar won the war, American production second, and the military strategy third. Seemed to want to indicate he thought the war was being lost until radar began to sink the submarines. (Fact or not, he was here, it seemed to me, excusing himself for saying the war was lost to the democracies, with the unvoiced appeal, how could he know about radar. I wanted to suggest any man of sufficient perception could have anticipated that the American machine would have come up with radar as well as production, but decided to stay mum.) To establish another point, that we were never sure of anything, he mentioned how surprised *Stars and Stripes* were when Churchill got licked. He was also making some point I lost about the English people.

O yes, and about the time he mentioned radar, he offset the BBC, and challenged the idea that propaganda had anything to do with the victory. "The shit of BBC."

Spoke of *Infantry Journal*, and said how superior it was to *Stars and Stripes*. Asked me if I had seen *S&S*. Said we over here didn't see it.

The two old ladies,[17] one 80, who came and sewed a patch for the shoulder of his jacket. And he worries over them coming, something about their car, and sense they can't do much.

Also, the way he introduced the clothes business. It would be an act of grace . . . and then smothering it, so that it wasn't begging, or perhaps too direct a request to me. Meanwhile fingering back and forth the ends of his shirt sleeves under his jacket, which appear to have had none, or lost their buttons. Actually he looks as a writer might working at his desk. I take it his worry springs from his normal fastidiousness about laundry etc. He mentioned how everything goes into service, whatever that meant. Spoke of his pajamas at Gallinger. He is neatly shaved, and his chin beard trimmed. His hair apparently is naturally tight and curled, and stays put.

Wanted to give, beside Cantos 50–61, his Kulch, as he called it, to the doctor. Threw in the remark, Laughlin dropped the K, as he explained he meant *"Guide.."* And indicated, I don't remember whether by words, Faber and Faber's part.[18]

The business of candy bars—"4 or 5 cents each." "Scarce in Italy." "A few dollars amongst my things at Gallinger."

I said I would bring my wife over one day, and said I imagined it might be pleasant for him to see a woman again. He agreed heartily, and said only the nurse at Gallinger, and somewhere, Pisa? some matrons whom he described in a spate of Italian, which I understood? to indicate some big horsey creatures.

Canto 2, January 15, 1946

He was clothed in a new suit—[from] Caresse Crosby[1]—a blue, looked summer stuff, and the gray cast to it went well with his redness. He comes forward with a movement peculiar to himself, both like a loaded gun and with the sort of blind swing of a battering ram. It is all upper body, a sense of chest and head. Part of it's restlessness to get things going, which accounts for a motion to the right and ahead, as though to hurry past one. And some feeling of anxiety that if he doesn't unload, he may lose what's on his mind. This comes out during conversation, and yesterday, after a spill on *Newsweek*, Rep Tinkham,[2] the indictment, and Westbrook Pegler,[3] he exclaimed, "My mind goes so fast—" and broke off. When Caresse Crosby saw him he stopped his talk for a second to interject: "What you are hearing is off the top . . . ," indicating his head. But it is the blindness which is the remaining sense, over concentrated, obsessional, rushing ahead of the reality, not so much of himself as of all else, impatience, impatience, impatience.

He plunged right in on some *Newsweek* article he had read about himself.[4] There ought to be some way to answer these things. (His way of suggesting things to me. On this I drew back, to keep clear of his politics.) He rushed on about the indictment, mentioning two Italian fascist officials, indicating again the same theme that he was working with those who were against Musso, mentioning one of them as apparently the guy who had to pass on the other side of the street to avoid the Boss's stink. Said the agreement clearly states he

42

was to say nothing that went against his conscience or that would involve him as an American citizen. Also asked that this business of his being paid for his broadcasts be answered.[5] I was withdrawn on all this, am, but my agreement came out when he said: "They don't understand over here, but the Italians do, that you have to consider these things in terms of *idea*."

If I remember correctly, he continued on with this, while I went back again into the back of my chair, asking what had happened to Tinkham, and saying something about him as President of the U.S.[6] I indicated I gathered he meant the Mass. representative, and he then asserted it was Tinkham who gave him his sense of what was going on. I didn't understand what he meant, asked him if he meant T personally, but he said, his letters to the Treasury(?).[7] He spoke of T in that way that a writer does about a book or individual who gave him a clue on which to build his work. It was that rare thing, respect for the work of others, which creates the sense of past, tradition, and out of which men like Yeats and Pound shaped authority as they understood it. Unhappily, in this instance, it's Tinkham, not Confucius.

He referred to some news items about banks, one recently showing 45% profit, another 56 or something. And was it in here that he asked, does anyone know Westbrook Pegler? I indicated I didn't, and must have froze more than I ever have with him. He then called him "the best man they've got." And with that, for the first time, the full shock of what a fascist s.o.b. Pound is caught up with me. I guess I had to feel it on my own America before I could have a realization. For Pegler I have traveled through and understood. Pound's praise of him reveals his utter incomprehension of what is going on, and what has happened to himself. Just on a technical level, that such an ear as Pound's could permit itself to praise Pegler! What a collapse. I wondered then how long more I can hold out my hand to him as a poet and a man. I suppose I shall tell him one day I am the son of immigrants, this influx of second class citizens whom

Pegler and Pound think has made impure their Yankee America of pioneers—and Biddles. That my father was killed fighting for the right of labor men to organize in unions.[8] That decadent democracy gave me the chance to grope out of the American city into some understanding of what life is, and how to peg a smart fascist s.o.b. like Pegler—and Ezra Pound. Meanwhile I shall do what I can, as long as I can, for this fool of hate because once he was also a fool of love.

The contradiction I am in here was exhibited all the time yesterday. Wherever Pound remained on the level of intellect and the creative he was dead right, as in his plea to discuss the war in relation to idea, in his insistence that the Gaudier Brzeska[9] drawings he wants me to tell Caresse Crosby are at Rapallo are the things and not the picassos and the rest which are bought, "the shit of decadence." Or "*View*,"[10] and "it's Europe 30 years ago, that cultural lag again." Right. That's what his examination of his world has brought him. He emphasized what was wanted, wanting, was vigor. Gaudier Brzeska. Indicated somehow, words or no, he died in World War I but was today more forward than any of the rest of the shits who sell.

But wrong with a stink of death on all to do with politics and society. Here a fascist as evil as all of them. The confusion of the people with decadence. So that they become his and Pegler's mob— to fear, and thus to hate. The filth of them both, the bastards, and Pound the worst, for the brain and the ear and the flesh to know better. Cut off, he is, cut off from life. That a poet should choose hate!

The curious thing in all this is that everything Pound has to say and feel *politically* is what *View* is *artistically*: 30 years old and dead as a duck. He talks about the middle of the century just as young pacifists did the first world war. It is clear he only experienced war and politics once: in England, World War I. And the sickness he describes in Mauberley, "the modern man in the city feels, or perceives it as the savage in the forest,"[11] became Pound's sickness— and he suffers from it today. Maybe it was accidental, but the conjunction of Gaudier Brzeska's death to the whole conversation appears to me to be important. It is as though Pound has never got over it, that Gaudier's death is the source of his hate for contemporary England and America, that then, in 1915, his attack on democracy got mixed up with Gaudier's death, and all his turn since has been revenge for the boy's death. The result, he stopped short then, and has never advanced. It is like an old anarchist I know,[12] who was sent to Siberia in the 1905 Revolution, and has never grown since that one flash of life at 25. The result is his hate for Czarist Russia got fixed, and today he automatically hates Russia as Soviet, Stalin as ruler, and all which has to do with Russia since 1905. Or like Burton, who is a fascist, in some way because he hated war, I should imagine due to some shock connected with World War I.

(I had to interrupt this record to go down town. While there I met Caresse Crosby to give her Pound's message. She had gone to see him at the request of the hospital staff who wanted to get the impressions of someone who had known him many years ago. And to her Pound seemed no different. She marked, as a sign of his continued coherence, the way he corrected her as to dates in the past over when, for example, she had published at the Black Sun his *IMAGINARY CONVERSATIONS*.[13] And others, concerning people or events they had known in common.

She told me she had stated quite directly that she knew nothing of his indictment and that he must understand that her coming to see him was no indication of her attitude toward the charges. "I spoke to Ezra quite plainly."

He spoke of his troubles to her, and she was impressed by one remark: "My mistake was to go on after Pearl Harbor."[14]

It also seemed wry to her to have him say: "It is a shame I am in here. It is a time when if I were out I could do so much good." I gathered that this is his SAVE THE CONSTITUTION line, he and Pegler. It prompts me to remember Greenberg's analysis,[15] that my demand for a judgment of Pound by the writers as a writer must not be misunderstood, that two other things must simultaneously go on, his trial for treason, a judgment of him as fascist, as well as a total picture of what he was and how he came to be what he is. It is clear to me after my conversation with him Tuesday that I stand for keeping him in custody, or if released, he be under the strictest of control. If I were laying out a plan, I should immediately put him in some less enclosed place, give him privacy and simple care, books and paper, and freedom to continue his literary work. This could be done within the framework of the Federal prison system, if it were recognized that the rehabilitation of such a prisoner as Pound includes allowing him to work at his "trade." There is no need in his case to teach him basketweaving, machine tooling, or carpentry. His craft is there, and society can still use his gift for language if it wants to. A translation of Confucius could be a fruit of his imprisonment. Otherwise he is all waste. But he should under no circumstance be given any freedom which would allow him to do what he called to C. C. "good."

We station soldiers to see that the Nuremberg prisoners do not commit suicide. Why can't we create conditions which will prevent the loss of Pound's lines? They are as useful to society as the Nuremberg lives, without regard to the individual Pound or Goering. In one case we keep them alive only to prove their guilt, in the other we neglect his gift. It is his own remark to correspondents at Pisa: "If I'm of more use dead than alive, that's that."[16]

As things stand now he is not doing a bit of work. His mind flies off. He told me Tuesday he had read some work by the author of *The Harbor*[17]—and that was as much as he could do. He said that it had been hard going for him to get through Ann [sic] Rand's *Fountainhead!* Apparently newspapers, and magazines, are about his limit, and even here I have no way of knowing how he reads them. I imagine the doctor does. (It occurs to me: does Kavka keep a record of his talks with E. P.? If not, perhaps he would if I suggested it. It would be of interest to others, because of what Pound has stood for as a poet.)

His remark to C. C. about Pearl Harbor reminds me of what he said to me: "*If I had only read Confucius earlier I would not be in this mess.*"

At one point he again took a swipe at the British. He was rushing along about broadcasts, and pointed out that the British allowed only sets which picked up medium wave to be sold. The result was they did not have to worry about short wave reception. It seemed to me he was indicating that the Americans, because they weren't so smart, did worry and the result was Pound was here now in prison! He made some crack about if Joseph Priestly made some remarks Americans didn't like, they could shut him up. It was then he said: *Yeats said to me once, England is the only country in the world in which a man will lie without getting paid for it.*[18] And he went on, "But of course Priestly gets paid in other ways, he's a part of the gang." Somewhere in all this he again spit out: "The BBC. . . ."[19]

Apropos of America too, he said take Van Dine. No not the mystery writer. When Van Dine was called up for service in the last war, meaning I, he made some objections to an examiner, (Pound then shifted his voice to a tough's) "God damn you, don't you know no goddamned fool has no goddamned rights here."[20]

In a wish to see if there could be some coordination of what I might do for P and what others were doing I asked him if Cornell or Laughlin had been to see him. He said no, he had had a couple of postcards, they were off skiing somewhere. He then said I was his only anchor to windward. He said he couldn't expect much of the (Royall's?). The two 80 year old ladies who came to fix his coat, they were too old.[21]

He asked me to write his daughter and tell her he was no maniac, and not "repulsive." I asked him if he had heard from them, and it seemed he had had a letter from them written in October.

He jotted down fast the addresses, and kept talking of Mary's uncle (Ted?) (or was it as C. C. suggests, Tate, who wrote *SAVAGE MESSIAH?*)[22] In any case he did say Ted had seen the Gaudier-Brzeska's at Rapallo. He regretted he had never had the place or means to mount them, went on to indicate how they should be mounted, space mainly. Also, wildly jotted down two mss for Laughlin's attention, Mary Butts' *The Death of Felicity Taverner* and Ron Duncan's *Husbandman*.[23]

At one point he pulled up the top of his drawers and pointed out he had now to wear them all the time, night and day, because his things hadn't come from Gallinger. I said I had spoken of that to the doctor, and that the delay was one normal to government, in or out of prison. Asked me, the next time I came, to bring him a pair. I said how hard it is to find them, in wool. He asked for an old pair of mine. I said I didn't wear them. Then we got into a question of size. I figured he had a 36 waist. Which was my own: saying, you can't be bigger than me. He made as if to measure himself. No, not any bigger than you!

One other thing I remember from the conversation—and it floored me, as did the Pegler praise. "The only good thing on me that I have read," said Pound, "was the Austine Cassini's article!"[24] When he comes out with these cracks it takes me several seconds to believe my ears, I'm that naive and unprepared for the collapse of judgment brought about by hate. It flashed through my mind what he must think of Bill Williams or myself on him! And how all he wants is the purring and tears of fellow fascists. Who value him not one spit, and speak of his case with sympathy only to use it—and him—for typical fascist destructive purposes, to undermine the people's confidence in their society and its justice. As did John O'Donnell,[25] one day. I did not happen to see Austine Cassini. But it is not hard to imagine what she had to say. Poor, poor Pound, the great gift, the true intellectual, rotting away, being confined and maltreated by the Administration. SHIT. And he is taken in by it! Here he's a punk like the rest of them.

I must confront him again soon. Already this second experience is corroding my will to help him. And if it means I must withdraw my proffered hand, it better be soon, the sooner the fairer to him.

Or manage to steer the conversation into those things that I am interested in, and away from his fascism, which is a bore anyhow. He and all of them fall to type. It is only in the creative that he still speaks with individuality.

Canto 3, January 24, 1946, 3:10–3:30

Today's meeting was completely different in tone. It is strange, but the only word is gay. Right from the start it was wild and strong. I brought myself forward more, and Pound did too.

This time we were in the second of the two visiting cubicles, and the stair didn't spill away behind me, he was backed up by the heavy ward wall, and it seemed to create a more explosive character to our meeting. The guard was different too, less interesting than the regular one, so we sort of forgot him. Except when Pound, as always so instantly gracious, was quick to suggest he have a cigarette as I was opening a package to give one to Pound. The guard declined, and with that Pound says, CHAW CUT PLUG. And repeated it, CHAW CUT PLUG. Explaining to the guard he meant that's the only thing he guessed the guard did. The sudden explosion of Pound's voice in this phrase was quite total to me. It was the poet making sounds, trying them out to see if they warmed his ear. But it was the fascist too, as snob, classing the guard. And it was Pound's old spit at America. Add an ounce of courtesy in it, and you have something like what I mean.

I had provoked this tobacco business when I gave Pound the dates I had brought. Connie[1] and I had wondered if we couldn't bring him some of bertram's stuff.[2] So I asked him if he smoked. He said no, it made him nervous the next day. Then quite soon after, when he was rubbing his forehead with the heel of his hand, troubled by his lack of ability to concentrate, he had asked me for a cigarette,

50

which he smoked like a woman who does it to be free. But this is where the business led:

From cut plug, Pound suddenly said: "I suppose if I had used ————, (a brand of plug, I gathered, which I didn't catch) I'd be a Senator today!" It was too much for me! I said, "But you remember, Yeats warned you about that. Do not be a Senator, he said in the Packet . ."[3] Pound didn't say anything, looked at me sharp, and I went on: "That remark always seems funny to me, the difference between an Irish senator and an American is like a . . . planet . . . . . and a pumpkin." And then Pound, quite seriously and up out of his depths said, "I guess I never understand that." As though it had been a mistake of his. Of course what he was feeling was revealed in what he then launched into, a swift autobiography.

Before I record it, I should say that it was prepared by my chance meeting with Miss Maple, one of the two old ladies who have been also visiting him. While I was waiting downstairs to go up to visit, she came down, and asked the guard who it was that was waiting to see Mr. Pound. He pointed me out, she asked my name, said are you a journalist, I said no, a poet, o, she said, that's different, I said, He looks good physically, don't you think, she demurred, and was thinking of him when she saw him in 1939, and all the years back. I asked her how long she had known him, she said all her life, that is since 1906. I said, most of his life then too. I said, did you meet him in Idaho. And then she almost querulously corrected me, by explaining that it was an accident he had been born there, that it was because Pres. McKinley had sent his father out to survey the territory, and that Pound had actually been brought up in Philadelphia. Then, as people will, when they want to establish the propriety of someone, she started to tell me he had gone to Hamilton, Columbia . . . .[4] I indicated I knew of that, at least. She sort of muttered, "Even then he was unusual." There was distress in her, over his plight. But an air about her at the same time, which her visits prove. She asked me a strange question, Was I English? I answered no, American, and perhaps because I had felt the sting the last time of Pound's praise of Pegler, I went on, my father was Swedish and my mother Irish, which makes me very American. She looks up at me, and says, "Then you must have a sense of humor!"

The point is, I had recounted some of this, especially about my ancestry, to Pound when I had come up. He had apparently taken me for Norwegian. Said, apropos of her remark you are English, well, your face could be, and I said yes, I carry no marks of my blood, except possibly my height and there I outstripped my father. (It felt good to get the ancestry across to Pound for reasons aforesaid.)

So that there was preparation for Pound to go on from the Senator business thus: I was raised in an atmosphere of the civic Congressman. Of course I was only a child but . . . (Instantly the feeling of *Confucius* and his *Jeff and/or Muss.*)[5] My father met my mother here (Washington) when he was congressman. And after he was sent out to Idaho, he got appointed as assayer at the Mint. My mother tried to urge him to get out (and follow a career of public service, I gathered) but he refused. He was probably wise. He didn't say anymore, than I remember, yet I have the feeling of a large passage here. It is probably the intensity of Pound's feeling for civic responsibility, made painful now by where it has brought him.

His plea his broadcasts be examined is not without point. Wrong as he is, to my mind, in his conclusions on authority, and obscured, as fascists can be, by a mania to save the Constitution, no one can deny the seriousness with which he has examined civic responsibility. The personal sources of his obsession were revealed to me yesterday. It is a little like Biddle,[6] when I talked to him in his office, pointing out the engraving of Washington's cabinet, and proudly indicating his ancestor as one of the four. Though it must be said for Pound that his sense is not social, but societal, more John Adams, and the Adams' family sense. What's shallow about it is the deadness of it, the 18th century *lag* in it, the moan for the lost republican purity, the wish to return America to its condition of a small nation of farmers and city-state patricians, all Boston brahmin, and Philadelphia brick. Nothing wrong in that either, except what happens to political action now if it is so motivated. It turns out to be reactionary and fascist. For what are the positions it leads to? (1) an antagonism to immigration; (2) a hate for "foreign" elements; (3) a feeling of a Jewish conspiracy; (4) the old ways of "free enterprise"; (5) a Civil Liberties Union concept of the bill of rights; etc. In other words, a pitiful, sick and dangerous defense of all that *was*, which forever and anywhere and in all things, fears anything forward. Pound can talk all he likes about the *cultural lag* in America (he was at it again yesterday as of the Vanguard Press announcements, the 20 years lag) but he's got a 200 year *political lag* in himself. It comes down to this: a rejection of the single most important fact of the last 100 years, the most important human fact between Newton and the Atomic Bomb—the sudden multiple increase of the earth's population, the coming into existence of the *MASSES*. Pound and his kind want to ignore them. They try to lock them out. But they swarm at the windows in such numbers they black out the light and the air. And in their little place Pound and his kind suffocate, their fear turns to hate. And their hate breeds death. They want to kill. And, organized by Hitler and Mussolini, they do kill—millions. But the breeding goes on. And with it such social and political change as they shall not understand.

It is *economics* that finally confronts them, this science of the *masses*. And it is economic necessities which underlie the revolution in society and politics.

In Pound I am confronted by the tragic Double of our day. He is the demonstration of our duality. In language and form he is as forward, as much the revolutionist as Lenin. But in social, economic and political action he is as retrogressive as the Czar.

And then Pound jumped ahead to 1914 and Poland, and something about they were wise enough to get out. Or he was, I couldn't quite get it clear. (This date seemed to be important, for Pound there took a swing at the doctor Kavka, whom, he said, thinks that all my trouble starts there, 1914, Poland.)[7]

I believe it was here too that Pound said, "I told Potocki,[8] is that how you pronounce it? I said, Potostcki, and he went on, "I told him not to trust England." (Familiar?)

Pound's complaint about the doctor served somehow to create the gayety of the meeting, despite the anti-semitism which mixed itself into it. For poor Kavka does seem to be scared to death of this Pound business, and to be handling it in an absurd way because of his fear and uncertainty. God knows it is causing Pound a good deal of what I'm sure is unnecessary pain. He says Kavka keeps pounding questions at him . . . . and punched his fist against the wall of his other hand to illustrate the effect. He says he wakes up the following morning exhausted from trying to think back and work out the answers to his questions.

I tried to get him to take Kavka less seriously, telling Pound K is frightened to death, not of him as so much, as of the fact it is the Ezra Pound case. And that he's no more than a graduate student, trying to act professional.

At this Pound says, I never knew a doctor less scientific. If they want to examine me, why don't they give me some scientist, I wouldn't mind. He merely acts like a goddamn bureaucrat. But this intolerable questioning. Good god, what the hell, what the hell difference does it make what I was reading in 1902! (At this point Pound just continued to swear, and wondering if there was any "lady" in the next cubicle, saying he wouldn't want to shock them, he jumps up and looks around the corner, and finding none, continues to let it rip.

"With ANTISEMITE spread all over the front page of PM, you can't expect much else," he said, alluding to K., who was born Jonah Kafka, and is now Jerome Kavka,[9] as he told me when I gave him Pound's *Kulch* and *Cantos*—. (At that time K said, it hadn't made any impression on EP when he had learned his name was Kafka.)

Pound then followed up, "The other doctor I didn't mind." He meant Tiny, who had been in charge that one Sunday CC had visited. Tiny Ziman.[10] I point out to Pound that Tiny used to be a master of ceremonies in a night club, and had some experience of people. But that K was just a kid. Told him I had tried to get Tiny to bring K and me together informally.[11] And would try again. But that K has so far backed away from me. Probably K is also scared of that s.o.b. Griffin,[12] who is his boss.

Pound said, "They (meaning jews) were nice to me at the DDC[13] (jail?)."

"I guess the definition of a lunatic is a man surrounded by them."

He was quiet for a minute, working his forehead, when he started out, talking down and away toward the window to his right and my left: "There was a Jew, in London, Obermeyer, a doctor of comparative . . . . . of the endocrines, and I used to ask him what is the effect of circumcision. That's the question that gets them sore," and he begins to be impish as hell, "that sends them right up the pole. Try it, don't take my word, try it." And then, with a pitiful seriousness, turning directly toward me and says: "It must do something, after all these years and years, where the most sensitive nerves in the body are, rubbing them off, over and over again." ((It was fantastic, again the fascist bastard, the same god damned kind of medical nonsense Hitler and the gang used with the same seriousness, the same sick conviction.)) It was so cockeyed for the moment it was funny actually, absurd, and I was carried along by this swearing, swift, slashing creature.

I record it, but here as elsewhere, it is impossible to give a true impression. For at any given point, always, there is the presence of the seriousness of the man. Even in his sickest and most evil moments. He is always a man at work, examining, examining. Here, for example, on the one hand he is attacking K as a Jew, when the truth is K is making the mistakes of any young man, and Pound is

god damned well lucky it is K and not the monster Griffin who is
questioning him, is in charge. I could not help feeling during this
whole line of Pound's, how it was precisely the Jews around him
here and in the DDC[14] who gave him some warmth and help, how it
was through Tiny and K that I had got drawers issued to him, how it
was K who at least had the curiosity to read his verse, and that K, in
Chicago, when the bookstores said, they wouldn't carry the books
of a fascist, objected and damn well told them that was the same as
burning books, and plain out and out fascist. On top of that that it
was Rahv,[15] another Jew, who had accepted my Yeats thing on EP,
when all the blessed Christian editors took it as offering Pound an
out, an intellectual excuse.

Hate blinds. It makes this man of exquisite senses a false instrument. It makes a lie of perception. It empties Pound as completely
as Oscar's pitiful ego prevents him from any illumination of the
human beings around him.[16] Where all that Oscar takes in has to
come by way of the brain, as though he were some cathode tube without eyes, ears, skin to record, flesh to touch, Pound is become the
same thing in reverse, with eyes, ears, touch gone, and only gangren-
ous bowels left, rotted from fear, and giving off nothing but the
stink of hate.

Yet you see this isn't all, despite everything. For Pound will
spend his night honestly seeking answers to K's questions, genuinely
trying to give this Jew what he wants. He will appreciate Tiny, and
the others at the District jail. He will mention his debt to the Jew in
Rome who suggested to him to translate Confucius. He remains, on
the creative side of him, whole, and as charming and open and warm
a human being as I know. Despite all the corruption of his body
politic.

It is this contradiction which keeps me from turning my back
on him. I imagine that is why when suddenly he throws his bowels
in my face I am forever surprised and react too late for anger and
disgust to strike back. I am carried on by the gravity and intensity

of the man, now as ever examining, examining, as puzzled as ever to the questions, as naive as your skin and mine to a new rain, an open man, the poet, who does not hide his pain, joy, doubt, pride,—or hate. Sick he had made himself, finally a menace, yet point by point, cornered as he is, I shall still hold out the hand.

He gave me a chance to catch up with myself at one point yesterday, when he again mentioned Austine Cassini. It came early in the conversation, when he said: "It is time someone examined my broadcasts." He had in mind a defense, in the press. I was again off guard, in this instance, because I go to Pound as a writer and go on the assumption we can talk without this trial coming in. Which is of course utterly silly. And ignores the fact that Pound has nothing else on his mind. Anything else is accidenta, and leads back in any case to the sore place inside him. So all I said, was, weakly, "But I don't think they are available."[17] He said, yes, and mentioned the name of some woman who had examined them. It was then he asked if anyone knew Austine Cassini, and quickly said, But I mentioned her to you last time.

This time I couldn't let it go. I said, Such people are not your friends, Mr Pound. They do you no good outside. For their interest in your case is false, and they misuse you. They have not examined things as you have, lack the intellectual grounds you establish. (God knows I felt as I said this that to him, alone and isolated in prison with one thought only, how to get out of this mess, an Austine Cassini or a John O'Donnell are the only ones who appear as friends. And I also thought, yes, and in the straight fascist sense, they are your friends, and the only ones. And I dare say my sense of a total Pound, or Bill Williams, doesn't mean, now a goddamnedthing to Pound, really. But there it is, I am the friend of the man. (When I signed the register, the new guard couldn't read my name or the word "friend" written in the space for relation, and interrupted to say, are you his brother, was it?)

I went on: "Actually, your sense of the civic responsibility is the strongest base on which your case rests," contrasting it by the tone of my voice to the Cassinis and Peglers.

I paid him one compliment, when he complained he couldn't concentrate, and make a coherent conversation. (It was about this time he asked for a cigarette.) Actually, in these conversations, he has seemed to me to be quite coherent and consecutive, and I said so, in hopes he would take the judgment of someone outside himself, someone admittedly "fresh" to him as myself, but a reasonable judge. He made nothing of it, as he doesn't of any remark to him, actually. You can see him take such things into himself, and know he hears, but that's all. The only instance I can recall now where I did get an immediate response was on the difference between an Irish and an American Senator.

When he was sounding off about the doctor, he plead convincingly that what he most needed was to be led away from the subject of himself, to be given rest from this question of why he was what he has become, just the opposite of what Kavka was doing. It was then he said, "Ford, I happened on a novel of his, and it did me more good than anything has, to restore me, except Katherine." It turned out he meant FordmFord's *SO* . . . . ,[18] for as I was leaving he said, read it, the second volume isn't as good as the first, but I had forgotten what a fine novelist he was.

I asked him: "Katherine?" He said: "O, Katherine Proctor, didn't I tell you about her visit to me at the Jail. Yes, I've known her for 40 years. Of course then she was full of Wellesley and that stuff. But she had married the man who did the stained glass windows in the Cathedral here, and had done nothing all these 40 years but read the Bible. Of course it's Bibles only that I have had. First, it was a Jewish Testament, the manual they use in the Army. Then a priest brought me a new Catholic version, a little bigger, but the translation not as good as the old Version. And then the regular one bigger than that. I had a pile so big it crowded what little room there was on the table beside my cot. So in comes Katherine, with a couple of her fat children, to reform the old reprobate, to save the sinner's soul, despite the fact he might not want to be saved. (Laughing, laughing, full of red-beard, redhead, red tongue laughing) Swearing, slashing, but at the same time telling how good it was to see her and why it was she and Ford only that have done anything to give him rest and restore him to some equanimity in the midst of these, his troubles.)

I can't for the life of me remember what it was that provoked the 20 year lag again business, but he said, indicating with his hands the closing of a gap, "I have tried to bring them up . . . ," meaning even with themselves. Then he, why, I don't know unless he has just seen their catalogue, but he says: "Look at Vanguard's List, just look at it, don't say anything, just look, and then Vanguard's list 20 years ago.

As of dates I brought, "I eat anything."

As I was leaving half to me and half to the guard, swearing away, he was half complaining, half laughing at the way the whole ward and its troubles seems to have to go through his room, by his door, illustrating "the poor guy in the next cell" by suddenly going down on his heels, and squatting all bent over, his hands over his head, as agile and quick as you please, a Kollwitz pose of misery. And coming up, saying "And Wahoo," meaning I suppose the Indian who talked about bumping off 10,000 people.

I had assumed he was in an open ward, but he spoke of the heat apropos of my telling him I couldn't get him long drawers, there were no wool ones, saying he didn't want wool, too hot, they keep the . . . . . (some hall) too hot. I asked about the courtyard for walking and he said, horrible. Then he told me he had a room to himself and all the ventilation he needed. "Only if they wouldn't have to lock the door at night. Of course I'm getting better. I only have to go to the toilet two times now."

I told him I had seen CC and reported on the Gaudier Brzescas. He said, yes, and launched again into what he would do with them:

"I'd put some 24 of them up in a large room like a frieze." I said, "How many of them are there anyhow?" And he, indicating piles, said, "All his charcoal drawings. She ought to be able to sell them to some gallery . . . ."

I said, "You make Gaudier seem so young"—and I went on with what I have thought so often, "as you seem to me yourself, so young." And he crushes his head and face in his hands, and says nothing.

Canto 4, January 29, 2:55–3:15

I had a sense of pressure right from the start. Pound was wound so tight when he came in I felt anxious for him, almost feared he might snap. "So good of you to come" (putting his hands over mine on the table). "King came to see me yesterday" (to my question said he was Control Officer for Justice)[1] "and he sees I could be of use." "When I heard of your sanity trial tomorrow . . ." "Yes, I was examined by 6 of them yesterday." (Which probably accounts for the tension!) I reported I had talked to Kavka and the questioning was now finished. It was the visit from King which set the tone of the short time we had together. For Pound was off like a runaway horse at the assumption that King seemed sympathetic and gave him the impression he might get out, be put to use.

The use, of course, is no longer his writing, but saving the world by stamp scrip. "I could do so much in Italy, yes, and Germany too, where they know me." Then he went on about those who merely carry rosary beads, mentioned some Italian who tended his garden so carefully he watched where each olive tree would grow. It seemed this man was going on pilgrimages to Monte Allegro.[2] I gathered that somehow this was proof of how Pound was revered. "These people who know me, have lived with me, know I'm not suspicious," (to be suspected).

He shot in something about "I understand they think to send me to Japan. I could find out things, what the Russians are up to. . . ."

61

Back to Europe and Italy. And again the fixation: learning Georgian and going to talk across the board to Stalin. "They send some pot-bellied millionaire." (Gesture of five fingers off the nose.) "What the hell does he care for what he knows to be a capitalist sow, the like of which, plenty of 'em, he bumped off plenty of times in Tiflis. Send a lunatic like me, take a different line, Barkov would have arranged it. But ten months are gone." (Feeling we better get to it, another day wasted is too much.) "Barkov,[3] Frobenius[4] and I. . . . Barkov said to me the first time we met" (with that a swift French, too swift for me to understand). "I don't know where Barkov is or what he is doing, but I saw he received some guest at the Moscow Station. Probably he's some undersecretary. He survived all the purges. I remember saying to him in Italy: "Now, is there any difference between what we've got here and what the Russians have with the Bolsheviks." This time, a French which he translated for me: "It belongs to them." Which reply of Barkov seemed to Pound to cut through everything, to be the balls of the thing. Giving the impression you can deal with men like that, meaning Stalin. Then Pound makes clear this: "I was always a Stalinite, no Trotskyite."

In the midst of this a recollection of Paris, and how it was Barkov that got EECummings into Russia. Said Pound: "I had had a letter from the *New Masses* asking me to do (an article? make a trip to R?). When EEC had difficulty getting a visa, I showed the New Masses letter to Barkov, said "Look here, here's a guy who is o.k., will do a good job." And that's how Cummings got in. The *New Masses* gang were sore as hell at me . . . (indicating he didn't know why!).

The King visit prompted more. He said again, but this time with more urgency, he thought things ought to be getting done, meaning, I gathered, the exigencies of the broadcasts, and also the answer on the pay business. "I think he would like to see me out of here," gesturing toward the barred window and the 30 foot wall outside.

He started talking about Dalton.[5] That if they sent him over he could talk to Dalton. Explained that when he went to London to close up his mother-in-law's house (1938) because Mary [i.e., Dorothy] was too sick to go, he had found pictures of Mrs Dalton from the age of 2 up. He had called her to ask if she wanted them. Said no, . . . and with this Pound tried to explain why he had not come to know the Daltons better. As if, however, that didn't matter, he still could make contact. I told the story of Dalton's new stand with Cripps against Bevin and the appointment of a new Chief of Foreign Affairs, a Dalton man, that D appeared to be emerging as the strong man.[6] Pound said: "Yes, he's the best man they've got."

This started him on the money business. "You see, most of the time shifting documents to the India Office. The family an old India family, proconsuls from way back. Her death was the first time any-thing fell out to us. We had money from then on. Fortunately the freehold was not hit in the raids, even though all around it was. So Mary [Dorothy] and I . . . that's the answer to whether I worked for pay. Don't get the impression Mary [Dorothy] had anything before, or that when I married her. . . . " (As far as I could judge, trying to convey to me it was not true he did marry for money!) "She had 750 a year.[7] In (was it 1924?) an uncle or something left her a little. But we never had much, enough to take care of the over-head at Rapallo, that's all. What I made, we spent . . . " (pleasures, luxuries). All over this mother-in-law business the sense he didn't have much time in London to do what he could have, a sense of regret now, that he hadn't mixed in and got some politics done, that he hadn't executed a Mission to London, through his stay, despite that, he could now follow up for the U.S.

He told me he had received another letter from Mary (14 days later than his last letter, and that she had written to Cornell and the Jail, St Elizabeths), and that Omar was at Rapallo, and full of filial feelings for *both* his parents (with a better indication of where the father was). Something about Omar collecting Durer, started by his uncle, hers, Tucker[8] the first to make a big collection . . . (At this the usual collapse of his face into worry and concern, and an intense impression of helplessness, caught as he is in this snarl.)

Somewhere along in here, he suddenly said: "I had in mind to cry out in court: England has diamonds and emeralds!" I was at a loss to understand, until I caught on he had switched to the pending British loan. It is often so: he keeps reading the daily papers and suddenly bumping out of the line of conversation into a reference to the news. (It brings to mind what Kavka had to say about his broadcasts when I talked to him Tuesday on my way over to visit Pound. K said he was glad he hadn't read them until he had finished his questioning of Pound. He made the point that P's generalizations got pretty ugly the moment he broadcast and day by day introduced the topical, especially his attack on individuals and specific analysis of running events.)

"Of course the diamond market is rigged," Pound went on, "but emeralds still have a value for themselves. Britain not only needs no loan but could herself be making money." I gathered by selling her emeralds and diamonds, then putting the money in circulation via Pound's stamp-scrip.

It was here that he swung off into the higher mysteries of his economics and I came along behind, panting. Something about the Pennsylvania Colony having no debt as late as 17—. And Maine at one time when it got some money from the Federal Govt using scrip. Then Douglas and how his A + B thing was utterly true.[9] Even Douglas didn't know the Moslem ———— had used it.[10] Until he saw I was lost, and asked me, "Do you understand about stamp-scrip?"[11] To which I answered: "Only as I have read you on it!" Which jumped him quickly into a simplified explanation: "A dollar bill. Each month you put a penny stamp on it. Thus each year the Govt. gets 12% back on its money. And it should: it does certain things to put the money out and ought to get some return." Instead, if I get it right, of paying money itself to bankers, BANKERS, those mortal enemies of E.P. and the PEOPLE!

He explained that Douglas didn't at first advocate such a plan. His idea was to pay dividends on the national income.[12] On Dec. 31 the national wealth would be computed. At the end of the year the increase of national wealth would be divided among the people in the form of dividends. Thus each would be paid and able to buy goods and services. (If I followed.)

Then it was Gesell.[13] How he had only lasted in the Munich govt in 1919 for three months because, though he went in with Communists, the roughnecks of the Party took over. Gesell managed to get enough of the politicians to justify him and escape with his life. But Gesell was a business man and knew what earnings and how stamp scrip would solve it all.

Because Gesell goes back to Proudhon, not to Marx. Proudhon ((ALL THIS IS SAID MUCH BETTER THAN I CAN REPORT IN *Guide to Kulchur*. I am merely indexing what now is on Pound's mind.)) on rents.

Then a little bit on what he himself had done. When I got in to Rossoni[14] (see *Kulch*)—who?—the Minister of Agriculture. He said the State couldn't use scrip but the Corporations (by his head telling me they existed and were big) could, perhaps.

That was about all that got tucked into these 15 minutes. He did refer once to Laughlin, that he should have brought the proofs for the *Confucius* but was sick or something. That he had been to visit last when Pound was being transferred from Gallinger. That he had apparently sent the books: "All the doctors seem to have copies —getting culture. . . ."

Complained of the maniacs all seeming to have [to] pour by his door. Apropos of this, as I was waiting downstairs to be allowed up a couple of steamfitters came through the iron door, and one as he was passed, turned to the guard and said: "That Pound looks about as he did when he landed at the airport. Course he's shaved and that beard of his looks better, that's all. But if they put the son of a bitch down in Ward 1 the young fellows would know what he'd done and give him the beating up he deserves." It was another one of those things which catch you, like the letter carrier at the coal yards the other week complaining because he couldn't get a delivery of coal in a day and snarling to the Griffiths man, "There must be a Jew in it somewhere." This time, however, I had wits enough to talk back: and piped to the steamfitter: "You call that democratic." He looked around and, to my surprise, said "No." And gathering he meant by young fellows the G.I.s they have in Howard Hall: I said: "Wasn't that what we were fighting for?" He went on out. As at the coal yard there was a Negro standing by whose silence in each case was overwhelming. Both veterans!

The fact that I was coming to see him seemed to move him very much this time. When he was leaving he spoke of it. I said I had little but an ear to lend. He inscribed two of his books to me, one with deep gratitude and the other "as is, my onlye sustainer," or so I read his scrawl.[15] And as he started toward the door, he sort of half said strong as of me.

This is the place to note down some of the things Kavka had to say in our conversation before I went over to Howard Hall. It appears Pound the last few days had been pouring it out to K on the next war, the clash of the two ideologies, America and Russia.

It appears that Pound had been dwelling the last few days on the next war, and boasting, as men will who seek to understand and predict developments, on his insight, how right he had been 20 years ago!

· K revealed that at some time Pound had been drunk when they talked[16] and had expressed himself anti-Dostoevsky.

Pound had also performed for K what he calls his YIDDISH CHARLESTON, composed originally for Louis Zukofsky. K says it is something! and regrets he didn't get a recording. A dance which Pound does, with gesture, movement, words.[17]

When I mentioned how Pound appeared to me to be trying all sort of keys to get out of his trouble, K said: "That's all right, but it isn't new. He actually was frightened by the treason business long before he was indicted. He seems to have learned of its possibility from the Germans and wrote a letter at that time to the Attorney General, anticipating and answering such a charge, explaining why he was not a traitor.[18] He got no answer."

*　*　*

Jongleur, now jangled.
And was your wish
a mere need to ring
and sing
be cap and bells
to a king?
in Provencal?
or Yeats old Rafferty?

to turn Rapallo
or Philadelphia back
to a Provence?

to be
Yeats' old Rafferty?

Charm, the snob's, wasted
in a world too fat with plebs

P shows the servant too, as
Yeats, and instead of families
and great estates, Pound
would have dictators and
missions for his place.

Speed to madness near allied.
The basilisk eyes for public
use, as open intimately as
a Negro's or a child's.

The imp, and scandalizer.

Canto 5, February 7, 1946, 3:15–3:30

Today Pound was in bad condition, his eyes worried and muddy, his flesh puffy and old. It appears again to have been too much "hammering" at him. He started out by saying: "4 medicos at me this morning."[1] I tried to suggest it might end once the sanity hearing was over. He said they had had him dressed and waiting to go all last Tuesday, even after the hearing had been cancelled, but no one apparently had thought to let him or Howard Hall know. As he said: "I don't [know] what goes on. Who to believe. Cornell writes that the hearing will be next week.[2] But what is going on." He kept rubbing his head upwards with his hands. Wrought up, until it would squeeze your heart of blood. For this is all unnecessary, all the result of the negligence, thoughtlessness, carelessness, let things drift. Laughlin has not come, has not sent him the proofs of the *Confucius*: "which is the base of my defense." And of course from his point of view— and mine—he is right. His defense is the intellectual grounds of his examination into what is wrong with contemporary whig society. His conclusions may be wrong. But the process is a thing to protect. Which when mentioned is laughed at, as K did, for no court will try him on such grounds.

He announced that the best defense of him had appeared in Farc's paper (?), a Gesell organ in San Antonio, Texas, though it was harmed by a confusion of Tremaine & Truman (?).[3]

Connie was with me, and we brought a bottle of wine, but he was not allowed to have it. I sought to get his mind off and back to

68

writing. Mentioned I had stolen a poem from him. At which he made a gesture like a salute with the right hand, as much as to say, take it away. I said it was King Tching T'ang's inscription, apologizing for my Chinese.[4] He expressed his belief again that the inscription was important, saying Confucius is not understood, that that's what he stood for. I said I had tried to give in English some of the effect of the ideograph by using the words bare: AXE TREE SUN, but admitting how difficult it is, though challenging him a little by saying he has as much trouble by using the Chinese character. I went on to make clear it was the only time I had rifled him, directly, anyhow.

He got on to the subject of the Cantos. I asked him which were the 10 he had done at Pisa. 73–83, the two in Italian, 71, 72 cannot be published in America at the present time.[5] One is Guido's ghost, and (Ambrogo[6] or something I did not recognize). They are buttressed in the Inferno. Pound kept emphasizing the way they back up against Dante, come from him, even to terza rima. And gave me the sense that only Pound of all Dante's followers have picked up where Dante left off. Not that Pound said any such thing. Perhaps it was just that his emphasis on the way he has in these cantos gone back to stem from the Inferno suddenly gave me the sense of an unused method. No, Pound put it in this way. He is himself excited at having rediscovered and used a Dante method. He especially mentioned the use of a ghost to speak, repeating Guido.

Then he made clear why they cannot be published now. Smothering the facts from the sailor who was the attendant today, he told Connie and me that one of the cantos contains the tale of a girl of Rimini who has been raped and who leads a company of Canadians who had asked to be directed to ———— across a mine field instead. She also was blown up, both legs off. But it enabled two German prisoners to escape. The payoff came when Pound says, "She was one of the resistance."

It amazed both of us. Here we were listening not only to a fascist, but the ENEMY! The resistance was patently the German-

Italian gang behind Allied lines. Pound was talking like no American but an out and out enemy. The strange thing was there was no awareness on his part that we might take this as what for the very first time I have seen: TREASON. There it was staring us in the face and speaking straight out bold. And yet let me record: merely there it was. A fact. I felt no surprise. Nor, I confess, did it shock and repel me as did his reference to Pegler or his antisemitism. I am bewildered. He makes no heroine of her. (One could not judge until one read the canto.) He told it as a tale of war. But he also told it as a deed of one on his side. These were soldiers who were fighting against the Axis who died because of her betrayal.

I asked him if he still intended his original schema, of 100 Cantos, and he said yes. In other words 17 Cantos remain undone as of now. He gave the sense of the Dante between as a returning theme. I wanted to go on and ask if Yeats' description of the form is accurate.[7] We didn't get to that.

At one point I told him that CC was going to Italy to get out an issue of *PORTFOLIO*.[8] (She had brought him over a copy.) He mentioned Gaudier again, and other Italian painters. It suddenly occurred to me he might have known Cagli. He said: "I think he tried to do a portrait of me, but it didn't come off. He was a Jew, wasn't he?" I said, yes, his mother was, his father a Milanese. P said: "He came to me from Rome. I think he was interested in me because he thought I was a Jew, my first name . . ." (!) I protested it couldn't be Cagli, for he didn't work that way. But P insisted he thought it was the same person, and that he was a man who made racial judgments! (Or a phrase similar to that!) (How about that!) I said, "A Chirico man . . ."[9] but it didn't register on P. I went on to say Ciano had confiscated his work and driven him out,[10] and that here he had gone into the Army.

Ford again came up—"Fordey," as P calls him. As of his influence on the new American novels. *Whistle-Stop*,[11] for example, which P thinks good "unless I have lost my critical sense" he observed, in one of the several examples of his collapsed present state. In fact the whole effect today was of a demoralized man. He had nothing but tatters of dignity left. It was all, cover my brother's nakedness, with me. Even his parting remark: "Thank you for coming. You have saved my life more than once. Come again when you have the energy." (!) It was very unpleasant. I couldn't say anything but: "I can hold out a hand."

At another point, he came up from his hands on his head, to sway out with, "I'm sorry to be so lachrymose."

On Ford he is bothered by some sense of guilt, apparently at either not having fought for him as a writer or for having attacked him, though he insisted—"no backbiting." Something in the Ford matter is bothering him. He again said *SO LET IT BE* is fine, the second volume,————,[12] not so good. But he kept reiterating: He knew how to write.

I told him the story of how I was impelled to write to Ford the night before he was leaving for Europe. How much it had meant to us younger men to have him in N.Y. Pointing out that only he and Bill Williams were there for us among Pound's generation. I did not realize at the time I said it that it was a sort of comment on Pound being in Rapallo, exile.

He mentioned Frobenius as another he had missed. I asked if F was alive. He said: "No, he had come to (France?) for his 65th birthday. (Apparently P had wanted to be there, and couldn't.) And died. There was some mention also of Yeats' death.

(I had been recording some passages from the Cantos the night before, and feel now the Canto on love is an intellectual performance, but the Artemis hymn against Pity is true,[13] straight out of Pound. He is a hunter. He is inside a man who enjoys to close & kill the game. His attraction to Confucius must be the old thing, what we all do, confuse our opposite with ourselves.)

Canto 6, February 14, 2:30–2:45

It was the day after the hearing which declared Pound mentally unfit for trial on charges of treason. He came in with his bounce back, carrying the Pisa Cantos in his hand which Laughlin had delivered to him this morning. He had already corrected the typed copies of Cantos 74 and 75 (1 page job with music) and wanted me to either send them on or put them in JL's hands if he were still in town. Which he was. And which I did later in the afternoon.

Canto 74 opens thus:

The enormous tragedy of the dream in the peasant's bent shoulders
Manes! Manes was tanned and stuffed
Thus Ben and la Clara a Milano
                        by the heels at Milano
that maggots shd/eat the dead bullock
DIGENES, digenes, but the twice crucified
               where in history will you find it?
yet say this to the Possum: a bang, not a whimper,
        with a bang not with a whimper,
To build the city of Dioce whose terraces are the colour of stars.
The sauve eyes, quiet, not scornful,
         rain also is of the process.
What you depart from is not the way
and olive tree blown white in the wind
washed in the Kiang and Han
what whiteness will you add to this whiteness
                 what candor?

"the great periplum brings in the stars to our shores."
You who have passed the pillars and outward from Herakles
when Lucifer fell in N. Carolina.
if the suave air give way to scirocco
OU TIS, ou tis? Odisseus
                    the name of my family
the wind also is of the process
                    sorella la luna
Fear god and the stupidity of the populace,
. . . .

    I had time to read the whole Canto and am impressed by the
way Pound as late as last summer in the tent at Pisa, after the Gorilla
Cage, had still all his old power and beauty as a poet. Some other
passages from the Canto follow, lines only, torn out of context:

that free speech without free radio speech is as zero
                    and but one point needed for Stalin
you need not, i e, need not take over the means of production;
money to signify work done, inside, a system
                    and measured and wanted
"I have done no unnecessary manual labor"
reads the R.C. chaplain's prayer book
(expressed in confession for communion)
. . . .
"of sapphire for this stone giveth sleep."
not words whereto to be faithful
nor deeds that they be resolute
only that bird-hearted equity make timber
and lay hold of the earth. . . . .

and so his mouth was removed
as you will find it removed in his pictures
                    in principium verbum
                    paraclete or the verbum perfectum
                    sinceritas
. . . .
when the cat walked the top bar of the railing

CHARLES OLSON & EZRA POUND

. . . .
("beauty is difficult" passage)
. . . .
in the stillness outlasting all wars
. . . .
lay there Barabas and two thieves lay beside him
infantile sinthesis in Barabas
minus Hemingway, minus Antheil, ebullient
and by name Thos. Wilson
. . . .
and there was a smell of mint under the tent flaps
especially after the rain
and a white ox on the road toward Pisa
                as if facing the tower,
dark sheep in the drill field and on wet days were clouds,
. . . .
(Joe Gould, Bunting and a third person as only these speaking)
. . . .
in light of light is the *virtu*
                "sunt lumina" said Erigena Scotus
as of Shun on Mt Taishan
. . . .
                OMNIA
all things that are lights
. . . .
Pisa, in the 23rd year of the effort in sight of the tower
. . . .
a man on whom the sun has gone down
. . . .
first must destroy himself ere others destroy him
. . . .
amid the slaves learning slavery
                and the dull driven back toward the jungle
. . . .
Lordly men are to earth o'ergiven
                these the companions:

Fordie who wrote of giants
and William who dreamed of nobility
and Jim the comedian singing[1]

The sense, the whole sense of this meeting was Pound in power,
anew. Flushed with his return to work. Full of plans to get on with
new things, now that his fate was settled for awhile.

He had one complaint, a fistula which I gathered had been
operated on three times, but continued bad because of sitting "two
or three hours on the concrete" (?).[2] And "I want to get out into
the yard," indicating the space inside the wall of Howard Hall.
Apparently walking in the courtyard is unsatisfactory to him. At
this point I believe it was he repeated his definition of a lunatic:
"an animal somewhat surrounded by Jews."

He was full of the need to "close the gap" in America. This
time I spoke up: "Work to do it, but don't expect it to be closed for
a hundred years more. It goes deep." In here he threw out the remark:
"Mussolini tried to push Italy too fast."

He gave up talking suddenly and said, "You talk. What exactly
do you do." I begged off, saying I was tired, too much doing this
week, that I was down like the earth waiting for the rain. But he
persisted, kindly. I said writing. He asked how Connie and I lived.
I said she worked, had to, with my income for '45 $60. He laughed
and said, "I got mine up to £200 once, then it fell off to £40 something, that was in the last war." In answer to further questions, I
said my book, *CALL ME ISHMAEL*, was not getting anywhere with
the publishers.[3] Told him of the new deal on it. He suggested I send
it to Eliot with a covering letter to Ron Duncan.[4] I thanked him. He
said he didn't think Duncan could write poems, but that Eliot had
liked his last play.[5]

Then we returned to America and I let go with my SPACE idea,
indicating it was why I wanted to get this book out. I quoted the
first sentence,[6] and went on to add I thought it was only the Indians,

and not Pueblo or Navaho, but Aztec and Mexican Valley Indians that had done anything with the cruelty consequent to Space. At that Pound exclaimed: FROBENIUS! I said, I did not know his work, only as I had it from him, Pound. I did not know of any translation. He agreed and went on about some guy named Fox who had been translating but the war had come along and, I gathered, Fox had died.[7] Later on Pound spoke of the 30 volumes and spattered off the German title which I missed.[8]

We spoke also for the market for verse and I complained there was no magazine which was a frame for work, that they all had political positions, and that such positions made it impossible to get your things published properly. I went further to say politics belonged below, not on the surfaces of policy. I said *Harper's Bazaar* was my best market. He said, what about *Esquire*. I replied I had just sent them something including a nasty thing I had done last year in Key West.

He too seemed to think JL was tied up with *VIEW*, and said he had called it "shit" to JL that morning. Went on to say JL had no flair as a publisher.

As of the psychiatrists, he said he always forgot the important thing to say to them until the next day when it was too late.

As of publishers told me the story of Kewpie Reynal[9] coming to him in Italy and offering $5000 for his autobiography, something like Gertrude Stein's etc. And how when he heard what would go into it, cooling off more and more. Calling him Kewpie didn't help. But, says Pound, that's what Morley had called him,[10] and I thought that was his name. But I've done that all my life, said the wrong things, and bring the whole fucking crockery down around me.

But I pointed to the Canto copy I was to take away and said so this is the other side of your sharp tongue.

He kept talking about me as a container for him, making this drawing on the envelope of the Cantos to indicate what he meant.

As of the two old ladies, the Maple sisters, he says "it's like trying to ride a cat!"

It was too bad we had to be cut off by the guard, for we were steaming along. I asked for more time but the s.o.b. went official on us. I told Pound when I would be back in answer to his eager question, for he wants me to pick up the rest of the corrected copy on the Cantos in order to send it to JL.

Saw JL, and he was all excited about the examination the day before, stating the discussion got to the point where they were asking: What the hell is reality anyhow.

As I was leaving him I asked how much the unfit plea had been planned. And JL allowed he had from the beginning thot the thing was to get P out of trial, the easiest way. He appeared to have been surprised they found him "insane." I demurred. But he came back with this remark: "But this morning he came up with a remark like this, over the Jewish question: "It's too bad, and just when I had plans to rebuild the Temple in Jerusalem for them." I said, sure, he's crazy like a fascist, but shall we put this on rational or moral grounds.

Canto [7] March 19, 1946

"Among the ruins—among the ruins, the most beautiful memory in the Orient."

"It couldn't possibly be megalomania, the animal is too big!"

Mallarmé: "If a man could lose his audience three times in his lifetime, ... (it would be good for his work). As of Pound's prose, which he agreed with me had emerged as a style in *ABC of E* and *Jeff and Mutt*, about the same time.[1] Some Galton, reviewer for London Times,[2] way back had predicted it, on assumption no style was the beginning of a style.

Grishkin: his mention of the photo of her in the Cantos Pisa. He found it again, and the stored-up stuff like an atom bomb, who? Astafieva, would have nothing to do with EP, robbing the cradle, but Eliot he brought together with her, the making of a poem, the only time he ever was the cause of it.[3]

(Of my question whether my mss Eliot could cotton to, "the old Possom has a conscience, and if he thinks he ought to publish . . ."

(Of my raising in Gloucester, he connects Eliot, I register complaint against E's use of Dry Salvages, "And he isn't through with it yet."[4]

Old Fordy (as of his reading of Bennett's *Old Wives Tale*— "good as the French"[5]—"I might have made money if my snobbishness, which was at its height, hadn't made me sneer at this commoner")[6] said he never could understand a goddamned thing I said.

78

(I mentioned what Ford did for Dahlberg, and D's inscription to F,[7] and P asked to see the book.)

He also asked to see the mss of the Melville, after I had mentioned again the space stuff, apropos of rereading the end of MD.[8] Explained I hadn't wanted to burden him. Would be excited to have him read it.

Spencer had written him. I said, I never could get along with him. He said: "I shouldn't think you could." Indicating something undone in him. I said, he never had been straight. Mentioned what he had done to El.[9]

Also, as of ballet, told him of my premier, and what I had done with Massine and Platoff.[10] He asked if the time was Stowitz,[11] whom Pavlova had picked up in a school in California. S had got tired of the Russian ballet, and had turned to painting. Had done one of Pound as Force. Had toured East as dancer, liked by princes.

P told me of a dance of Astafieva, spermatopyros, done in her studio, come down from Byzantium, the making of the seed of life, it turning into fire, and then the drinking of it. Maybe I was the only one to understand it. The female equivalent of sperm, whatever that is. Yes, the little English girl next to me did, she got excited.

A spate on the conspiracy against printing which he of course blames on the Jews. Started off with Cerf. Told of Cerf buying out the deluxe presses which were getting out stuff (in England—named them, mentioned the Jews in them, seemed to contradict his point, among them Zukofsky). Idea—the knocking off of first rate talent, to get mass sales.

Also swung out notebook on some French catalogue of stuff to be published in Canada, and reeled off names of French writers left out, including Goncourt, Gourmont, Flaubert? etc[12]—he had sent letter to Spencer about it. Warned me as us to look out for it. Spoke of *Little Review*, and pointed out no *LR* in this war.[13] Named the writers they had brought together. None of you know each other. I

CHARLES OLSON & EZRA POUND

spent my years introducing Americans to each other from Europe who lived on the same street. It was the same with my radio stuff. (Named two Princes, a Prince Dobrestoy[14] or something, some Italian professors, we were the only international culture hour on the air. On my Sunday hour I had them play Vivaldi until the disks wore out.

As I was leaving I said, pleased we had had over a half hour, it ought to be out of here and an evening, he turned toward the guard and said: "I ought to be out of here for the cultural uplift of the nation." I said: "This is the cultural uplift of Olson."

I had come to talk about my plans for work at the present moment. But before I could mention I was casting around he opened up again on Jefferson and Mazzei, said Splavin wasn't going to do it,[15] explained he had wanted me to do it in the first place. I indicated I'd look into it, but that I was thinking of something on the Cantos, as one of three alternatives at the moment. Then he reads me a lesson I had myself thought about as of him in the last week. Which was the J-M was the way to begin, three weeks job, chance to do a more solid thing than one could on other parts of the Cantos, as the Germans or Renaissance would do. As he had done on Cavalcanti, and Arnaut Daniel. Then—surprise—he emphasizes the use to me as a writer—publicity, your name on something, publishers, force them to do something else! Obviously his own technique. An introduction on the Mazzei translation—even if only 30 pages—connecting it up with the Siena Cantos. . . . Will look into it, I still indicated. And will. He insisted a job on the Cantos would be a long one.

I admitted it, owned up that I did not feel prepared to do it, any more than my other project, a long poem WEST.[16] (No response.) Said I had not yet accomplished the craft he had worked on when he was much younger. Acknowledged my respect for his insistence on craft. He said: "I'm only now beginning to reap the benefits." I said I took the line of the Pisas to be stronger than anything before. He said: "It ought to be that way," indicating why surprise. I said: "We have got used to men not continuing to increase their strength." It was then he quoted Mallarmé.

And when I roared over his analysis of the psychiatrists' trouble deciding it was megalomania when the animal was so great, he said: "It isn't time yet to laugh." I had to turn fast, and said: "I must, I will laugh, for I anticipate the returning strength (of the giant). I see it."

He rubbed his head about this time—as he does less now—and complained of his memory. I: "As Fordy, you now underestimate your coherence. Of course I can't compare it to what it was. . . ." And he broke in Among the ruins, among the ruins is the most beautiful memory in the Orient. I am convinced he did not say Occident.[17] (Just megalomania!) (megalolipsa)

Told me Laughlin had sent Kavka all of his works. I flashed out: "God damn Laughlin he'd send them to a doctor but not to me. I'm damn well going to take them away from K. After all I was the one who gave K your books to start him off. And Pound says, he had to pay $3.50 to the Yale Press for *MAKE IT NEW*, and it hurts him still!

I told him at one point I had read the *Capital Daily* '39 job,[18] and said it was a straight ball thrown. He said, he knocked it off in 15 minutes one day here. O.K. I liked it. It had the care and the speed. Later I mention it as of his prose, when he was talking about Bennett and novels and I allowed I couldn't read prose of such long wind. But he was talking about the construction, and praising it. I asked him if anybody had commented on his prose. He started out to say plenty, but I saw he meant the subject matter, and I stopped him, and meant as language, but that was the end of the interview. I had said tentatively I thought his prose had had more influence on me than his verse line as of now.

He gave me the address of Eileen Lane Kinney, 2301 Conn Ave, Co 5223, office 7500, ex 4825, as an old friend of his and Brancusi,[19] who had come to see him a couple of times. Suggested I look her up.

Abrupt: "I just thought of a phrase: America, where people listen to Freud and not to Frobenius." He may be right. I must get hold of Frobenius somewhere. Maybe parts have been translated somewhere.

I never did get a chance to mention the third project, the which I think is closest to my heart and my hand's skill at the moment. That's the book on the Human Body. A record in the perfectest language I can manage of the HEART, BRAIN, LIVER, KIDNEY, the organs, to body them forth, to give a full sense of the instrument of the organism, approached on the simplest of premises: viz., the BODY is the first and simplest and most unthought of fact of a human life. We assume it, are wracked by it, steered, moved from birth to death through it, and yet it never occurs to us to look down into it, to examine it as depths and function, to know it, as we do our trades, the outward realities. The whole job will take start from physiology, but be free of it from the moment of writing. I want to give a simple, straight, dramatic sense of the animation.

Maybe the whole thing will be merely the learning, in order to prepare myself for the fables of organs I have long wanted to do. But the project now is definitely to write the HUMAN BODY as object and function, without any interpretation and no soul stuff, just as simply as I tried to tell the story of what happened to the men of the ESSEX.[20] It is this: what happens within ourselves.

Pound. Healthy. Better. His door is open, he now is let into the moat. He is writing letters and reading Verlaine etc, not whistle stop. It is his slackening of memory that troubles him most now. Or so it was today. At only one point beside Cerf did he spill out the poisons. That was over the anti-semitism which he feels so many are now against him on. His remark today was: "Anti-semitism is not in the indictment!" It should be pointed out, he indicates. This silence, he murmurs. . . . I suppose I have to take it. . . . In this discussion, or in the Cerf thing, describing one of the printers, Goden was it by name, he characterized him as with talent, but with that "Jewish sterility!" There it is. It stops you. You feel him imagining himself as the last rock of culture and civilization being swept over by a wave of barbarism and Jews (communism and commercialism), the saviour of more than the Constitution, the saviour of all that has been culture, the snob of the West. For he is the AESTHETE, as I had Yeats speak of him. All—his pride in his memory, his sense of the internationale of writers, painters, musicians, and the aristocrats, his study of form as technique (no contours, no edges, intellectual concepts, but rounding, thrusting, as a splash of color, as Yeats described his aim in the Cantos, after Porteous disastrous painting) it is all a huge AESTHETICISM, ending in hate for Jews, Reds, change, the content and matter often of disaster, a loss of future, and in that a fatality as death-full as those for whom the atom bomb is Armageddon, not Apocalypse. Diablo, FORCE in Stowitz' wisps, the Mephisto of Fascism, the Fool of the Corporate State, Jongleur of Stamp Scrip.

Irritation at Laughlin's delay on the *Confucius*. Isn't it just him, as person, a drifter. No, everywhere, (what?) Frustration—a conspiracy of printers, or of those who boss the printed word. Some story of a Naval officer who financed the publication of *AMO ET ORO*[21] or something I do not know of P's. P told him: Don't ask the authorities for permission. Just publish it.

Damn if he may not be right. God knows I often feel there is a hand on the throat of all expression. The big machinery of the word, press, radio, movies is horrible. But as in so much, he fights as aesthete and as anarchist like Ed[ward Dahlberg]. I say, it is an interim, a death of 3000 years. I'll live on into what's coming up. Black as it is I'll keep red through it.

Laundry bag.

Grishkin.

He doesn't know whether his wife is coming, or just finding out if there is a boat by which she might come.

He gives the sense of Laughlin as the last hope here of publishing surviving the deluge.

Except for Goldring[22] he feels he said as much as anyone for Fordy. (Again the funny sense of guilt. As of Bennett, the wrong he did, mostly to himself. "He set out to write a great novel and did it as the son of a of course as the son of a storekeeper would.")

[Canto 8]
¼ POUND: April 30 (after five weeks): 20 minutes

preface by Joe Gould:[1]

> Ezra Pound lost,
> Is found
> Is not a hound
> His mind's unsound

key note by W. B. Yeats (via E. P., all smothered in his beard):

> You say, as I have often given tongue
> In praise of what another's said or sung,
> 'Twere politic to do the like by these;
> But was there ever dog that praised his fleas?[2]

"Fordie must be used, now he is dead, to take the lice off Eliot's back. Yes, I know Eliot is now paralyzed from the neck up: he must be to turn back a book like yours. But all the years it was Eliot who kept the lice off my back. And Fordie saw the danger of Eliot (meaning the fleas his hair would collect)." (At the moment I am covered with these fleas off Eliot's back, the little boys who preach "systematic criticism" against my work on Melville.)[3] Says Pound: "That ass Mathiessen."[4] But Fordie didn't know what to keep off the page. He saw the danger, but. . . . Now's the time to revive him. Stella (F's 2nd wife), before he took up with [words omitted] Biala,[5] says Fordie is being read again in England. 'Course Bill Williams will have to [be] sold on the idea it's the way to destroy Eliot. He will do any-

85

thing to get him; the trouble with Bill is, it's personal, not opposition. And there's Cummings: he would have a few sentences worth saying. And what about that novelist whom you said Fordie knew, Duisberg? (Dahlberg) I gave that *WAKE* no. on Cummings to Eileen (Brancusi's friend):[6] you and she make a nucleus for culture here in Washington."

(At this point I suggested P set down his feelings on Ford now he has been rereading him. Said he, "You can make a record of what I have said . . . . . thus: In detached and broken sentences . . . . Confucius said that after a man is 60 he is no longer active, but influences the action of younger men.

"Maybe Fordie did not understand me as he said he didn't. Now I know the guck over here I guess he didn't.

"It was . . . . . . who said that all a man has to say can be gotten on a half a sheet of paper."[7]

On Cagli: claims he was Zionist and stopped painting him the moment he heared P was agin' it; has idea C is very Jewish. "No more spreaders. You and I have a line together, culture. But here I am incommunicado, and I have to establish lines of communication.

On my book: he read me the riot act: "Don't touch the form as is, this book and Ron Duncan's the only two books we have. Make any additions the publishers want, as notes at the bottom of the page or as an appendix.

Goldring's *SOUTH LODGE*, on Yeats, Pound, Ford. P: "It was the high period of my life . . . . (or something like that, a sort of apology for his sentimentality about it, as he is reading it).

(His *use* of me: on his (and mine) series as spur to Laughlin and on circular to O'Donnell.)

[Canto 9] June 18, 1946: with EP from 1:20–1:45

I returned to see Pound yesterday. He has such charm. It is his charm which has betrayed him, for he assumes it can manage people. In itself, it is lovely, young, his maintaining of youth a rare thing. I do not know anyone who could be in a prison and stay as he: it was young of him, as Constance observes, to remark to Griffin, the doctor, as we spoke to him when he went through the visiting room yesterday ". . . before I got myself into this mess." As far as I can judge Pound acts within the walls much as he acted outside, the difference only of degree. Yet the Griffin incident also suggested the misuse of his charm which I feel has led Pound into snobbery, and the company of shits and fascists. It is clear he has Griffin pegged for the white trash he is. Yet he can traffic with him. And so that I shall not be misunderstood—Griffin is the boss of the prison—I shall also mention Pound on Ted Spencer, to whom he is not prisoner, and only beholden as he allows himself to be as writer to professor-critic. He told me Spencer had been to see him, and seemed impressed that Spencer could "take it," catch on when Pound told him "Eliot is fatal to you, Ted." I pointed out it was all intellectual with S, it would never lead to an intuition, point by point it could never form a curve when plotted which would lead S anywhere. So what the hell good was it? The truth is, S is flattered to be in the company of Eliot or Pound, without regard to life or feeling. It is a triumph for him, even to have Eliot fatal to him. That he should "take it" is all so kittenish. I told Pound what S had done to little Ellery Sedgwick, with his mean will, said El was the sweetest thing ever to come out of the old N.E. tradition. And Spencer bedevilled him. Along with Catholicism.

There is an assumption on Pound's part that he can traffic with snobs and bastards, and get away with it. I don't believe he or any man can, and I figure on this path he went to fascism. Or is it simply that he prefers such people, Princesses, and the rest of the fawners. For he has a hunger for power and name, and maybe he likes such creatures because somewhere in him unrecognized is a sense he never could make it. Maybe Yeats' warning: Do not be a Senator was more than an image, was a personal observation, and was meant to indicate to Pound: Reform it altogether.

The trouble with it is, he cuts the ground out of any relation. You come to distrust the nice things he says, look upon all his conduct as a wheedling or a blackmail. He becomes in fact not a Senator but a politician of friendship, and it's no good.

I enjoyed myself of course. For he is swift, and his wit is sure. He mentioned that Eliot was in this country. I said I understood one of his purposes was Pound. I said everyone in N.Y. and Cambridge was atwitter at his Second Coming, the Messiah, and that one of them, a publisher, as I remembered, had said his purpose was Pound. Pound smiled, turned himself out of the ease of the rocker he was sitting in, twisted towards the window and away [from] me, and remarked: "I have known Eliot for thirty years, and you are never sure. You know when he says 'No,' he won't do the thing, but when he says 'Yes,' you are never sure he will." It was a shrug, a tolerance, one of Pound's bites.

But there you are. The upshot of Spencer's visit was news a few days afterward from *WAKE* that they will devote an issue to E. P.![1] The politics pays off! As it has, so far as I can judge, during Pound's career. "They are doing Marianne Moore, then next spring they will do me. A daisy. It will be if I'm still around. What they regard as living!—Ford is a thousand times more alive than these living they want to celebrate!"

In Pound's case, however, I feel he has not cleared his course of the dangers. I think of the presence in his work of the worship for past accomplishments and a kind of blindness to the underground vigor of a present. Yesterday we batted around the radio, the movies, the magazines, and national advertising, the 4 Plagues of our time. I had in the morning, after Ziegfeld Follies, been wondering how deep the effects go, had recalled that, in time terms, the existence of these 4 was short, about the span of my own life, 35 years. I had been turning over in my mind how much actual rejection there was on the people's part, how much hope there was all 4 might in another measurable period be swept away.

Pound had made an observation about the expatriate, around the time we spoke of Eliot. Mentioned a story of James in which. No . . . . I remember. . . .

It was a pick-up on his part to my observation about Spencer. He went on to wonder if Henry Adams had the same intellectual complaint. We both admitted, of course, the difference in dimension. No . . . the Henrys have tricked my memory. . . . . .

Anyway, Pound spoke of a story of James', in which James imagines what he would have been like if he had not left his own country. *THE JOLLY CORNER*.[2] It was clear that Pound had been brooding (as much as he ever broods) about himself in this respect. I could not resist, because of some irritation I have with him over his politics, to say: "In your case what you would have run into around the corner was radar." He had in one of our earlier conversations admitted his surprise at it, and American production. It was his failure to calculate it that had led him to broadcast after Pearl Harbor, and put him here in St. Elizabeths.

It was a pleasure to listen to him on our Plagues, for he was talking out his direct impressions and actions, not going over into generalizations, so many of which or all of them become fascist and cliche. To suggest the difference from his usual dish, listen to this: "That Consummate Shit, in New York, on the radio, that provincial Winchell, how can people listen to him, no matter what he says, when they hear that voice. Their ears must be dead, if they can stand it." No crack at the Jew, no yaw-yaw, ja-ja, even the parenthesis excluding a measurement based on Winchell's doctrines![3]

It appears the fact the man in the next cell reads *Collier's* (the way it loosens, softens up the mind) etc all the time had stirred up this business, as well as Pound's hearing a Winchell broadcast on the radio. He said: "I first sensed it in 1910, when I made a crossing, and in the lounge saw men sitting around reading some 40 different magazines."[4] He went on to recall that he had been after it when he had first attacked Henry Van Dyke and *Harper's*.[5] (I gathered that was earlier than 1910.) Again I wanted to make him see the difference for us younger men, and why we don't arrive at the same conclusions as he does. I said: "But I, the men of my age, we didn't have the comparison you had to start with. We have had to work our way through, discarding each as we went, immunizing ourselves, the radio, the movies, magazines, advertising, until we came out to an island such as you started from." Pound: "Yes, Paris, the island, I called it, THE ISLE DE PARIS,[6] in an article I wrote then. Yes, Van Dyke was a daisy compared to the rubbish cans you men have."

It was fun to talk to him yesterday. He seemed in good health, and explained: "I've been all right since I got out of that courtyard." And he was. The conversation ran on, pushed against the guard who wanted us to quit. At the end I tried to get in this: "I've talked to a lot of the returning soldiers, and they seem to have come to rejections too, but the only alternative they grasp is the cynical."

(When we were discussing movies, he mentioned a film he saw in Italy on submarines, made by the actual officers and crews, which he said was fine, none of that poetic stuff, only one figure against the sky, and something about a review he [had] done about the thing, remarking that it was no wonder the director, ?Favellini?, hadn't any interest in movies, which the censor had scratched out so as to take the paper away. When I said it had not been shown here, he said O of course not, it must have been very liberated, destroyed altogether!)[7]

[Canto 10] February 9, 1948

"I don't know how to make you Americans understand that the earth turns around every twenty-four hours, and the work must get done."

"I don't want generalizations, I want particulars."

"You heard, of course, that Eliot has been raised to the peerage.[1] Bill Williams has done a good part of the job in Simpson's magazine, but it needs to be pointed out that the Areopagitica is as dangerous as the verse.[2] Eliot ought to get the Priz Nobel next year.[3] The goddamned Swedes wouldn't give it to him in 1943, saying it wouldn't be fair to award it to either side: at the very time Eliot's play was being produced in Italy, and the Italians would have been happy. (Mrs. Hauptmann told me Hauptmann changed the $40,000 into marks, and, says she, Mr Pound, they are worth one cent.

"No, they gave Eliot the O.M. Foch, Eisenhower, Henry James. Maybe they created it for James. He was on his death bed. They had to pin it on his shirt, or pajamas. Gosse. After they left, James, turning to the nurse, said: 'Nurse, draw the shades, draw the shades, it would be a shame not to hide my blushes.' "[4]

Moore.[5] Can't you get him to see Kirstein?[6] (Yes, but some of his friends on 2nd Avenue are closer to K than I am.) Yes, but I understand they are suspicious of your Scandinavian, Irish blood. (What goes? I first met Moore thru Cagli.) But you were hardly a Horn of Plenty![7] (At which point I also mentioned the Fasces.) ((The old man was closer to the mark.)) Only on this kosher subject (he

92

stopped painting me when he discovered my first name was not kosher) the old man makes me go blind.

E.g. Leite.[8] I had to spell it out for him, Leite was Yankee Portygee, and that he and I saw Jews and Negroes like Portygees and Italians, those who get pushed around. We don't like.

Which got P on to immigrant America. "Ya, they'll end up in sterilization. I was against passports a long time ago." At which I said, you were too late. If you wanted that position it had to be before the Civil War. Now we've got it to deal with. We are it, Leite and I and a few more. Sez P., well, if I was en retard, by 30 years, it's time we caught up!

Somewhere in here he pulled this: "I was a Zionist in Italy, but now I'm for pogroms, after what I've experienced in here (SLiz). Dr Rosenstock, back in Pisa, used to say: 'The Jews are stupid.' " All of which made me truculent. And more, sick of the bastard, and almost to the point of telling him off. Not him, so much as that [words omitted] wife. His hate is the horror of what is the kultur of this unfortunate day. Hers is just anglo-saxon fear and hate, the weak of the world who want, as ED once said, the liver of the Jew.[9]

Told him [the] story of that fucking whale,[10] and Duncan's phase, and Everson & Fabilli, and Rexroth,[11] of whose writing, says P, his writing is wooden and unreadable, instead of being as much in existence as wood.

Williams has been to see him, Arioste,[12] [Frank] Moore, and that seems to be the lot. He looks bad, his skin scaly, his eyes ratty, his beard sparse, his ass thick, his hair mothy. He feeds on hate, no question. His wife says the cold bothers him, even inside the jail. The truth is, the landscape of these grounds is as good as anything in America, god help us. Told him of El Granada,[13] as the only place where the shantied growths have not attacked like a piece of healthy skin left in an area of disease. And went on to spell out the economics why the Americans build so cheap and ugly. One has to with him. He makes culture conclusions. Like his racial ones. Bah.

GrandPa, GoodBye

1948

1

Time is in his conversation more often than anything else. I said to Lowell the other night:[1] "There is a haste in Pound, but it does not seem to be rushing to any future or away from any past." It is mere impatience, the nerves turning like a wild speed-machine (it is how he got his work done) and, more important, an intolerance of the mind's speed (fast as his goes), an intolerance even of himself. For he is not as vain as he acts. "30 yrs, 30 yrs behind the time" —you hear it from him, over and over. It is his measure (and his rod) for all work, and men. His mind bursts from the lags he sees around him.

He speaks as though he found himself like retarded when he began. Apropos Ford (F. M.), he said to me once: "From the intellectual centre, 30 yrs start of me."[2] He elaborated on it, another time: "Ford knew, when I was still sucking at Swinburne." (He credits Ford somewhere as the one who formulated the proposition, c. 1908: verse should be at least as well written as prose.)[3]

Now he puts all little magazines aside, or questions about someone's work, or presentation copies, with a jerk: "I can't be bothered. I've worked 40 yrs, I've done mine, and I can't be bothered trying to find out what the new candidates don't know."

"When I was a freshman . . . ," he started once.

2

If I were asked to say what I thought was the pure point of the Old Man as poet I would say the back-trail. The more familiar

97

observation, that it is his translations on which his fame will rest, is a step off the truth. They are a part of the career he has built on remembering, but the root is a given of his own nature. The lines and passages which stand out, from the start, capture a mood of loss, and bear a beauty of loss. It is as though Pound never had illusion, was born without an ear of his own, was, instead, an extraordinary ear of an era, and did the listening for a whole time, the sharpest sort of listening, from Dante down. (I think of Bill Williams' remark: "It's the best damned ear ever born to listen to this language!")[4] He said to me one of the first days I visited him, when he was in the penitentiary part of the hospital, what he has now come to call the Hell-Hole to distinguish it from his first detention cell at Pisa, the Gorilla Cage(where he felt he had been broken), "Among the ruins, among the ruins, the finest memory in the Orient." (He sd, "Orient.")

His conversation, as so much of the Cantos, is recall, stories of Picabia, Yeats (Willie), Fordie, Frobenius, Hauptmann,[5] of intelligent men, and it is as good as you can get. I was never made so aware of what a value he puts on anecdote as recently, when I returned from seven months on the Pacific Coast, and he jibed me, to what use I had put my time. I got around to my adventure in Hollywood, and young Huston's story of Jack Warner and the Whale. It pleased Pound much, and, as he sometimes does, wagging like an old saw, he says to Dorothy, "Well, seven months, one story, not bad, not bad at all. There aren't so many good stories after all." He's a collector—what's that line he had in the *Cantos* and took out, about scrap-bag, the *Cantos* as same?[6]

I dare say these are now commonplaces of Pound critique, but I don't think it has been sufficiently observed, if it has been observed, how much his work is a structure of mnemonics raised on a reed, nostalgia.

3

Edward Dahlberg has it, in *Do These Bones Live*, that ennui is the malaise of the life of our fathers, modern life I think he says, and in reference to Dostoevsky, and his women.[7] Is it far-fetched, or too easy of me to take Pound's haste, and this vertu of his verse, as born of same?

It is hard for me to do otherwise, having known him. His power is a funny thing. There is no question he's got the jump—his wit, the speed of his language, the grab of it, the intimidation of his skillfully-wrought career. But he has little power to compel, that is, by his person. He strikes you as brittle—and terribly American, insecure. I miss weight, and an abundance. He does not seem—and this is a crazy thing to say in the face of his beautiful verse, to appear ungrateful for it—but I say it, he does not seem to have inhabited his own experience. It is almost as though he converted too fast. The impression persists, that the only life he had lived is, in fact, the literary, and, admitting its necessity to our fathers, especially to him who had such a job of clearing to do, I take it a fault. For the verbal brilliance, delightful as it is, leaves the roots dry. One has a strong feeling, coming away from him, of a lack of the amorous, down there somewhere (I remember that Robert Duncan, when he returned to California from his cross-country pilgrimage to Pound, spoke of this, was struck by it.) E. P. is a tennis ball.

(When I think of what I have just said, and of those early poems!)

An attempt like this is such a presumption: said Frederick of Prussia, "Every man must save himself in his own way." You might say I am offering these notes out of curiosity, on the chance that they may or may not illumine him. He can stand it. He's no easy man. He has many devices. And he's large. I'm not sure that, precisely because of the use he has put nostalgia to, and the way he has used himself, he has not made of himself the ultimate image of the end of the West. Which is something.

(I am reminded of a remark of—I don't remember which, so help me, Lao Tse or Confucius!, that a shrewd man knows others, a true man illuminates himself.)[8]

Wait. I think I've got it. Yes, Ezra *is* a tennis ball, does bounce on, off, along, over everything. But that's the outside of him. Inside it's the same, but different, he bounces, but like light bounces. Inside he is like light is, the way light behaves. In this sense he is light, light is the way of E. P.'s knowing, light is the *numen* of him, light is his way.

And that is why he goes as he does, and why he is able to make his most beautiful poem of love later than "Cino,"[9] not so different from "Cino" either, but vastly more complete, and make the whole Canto—I am referring to XXXVI—a straight translation from Cavalcanti, the Cavalcanti itself one whole extrapolation of love in terms of light, and drawn, in its turn, straight from Grosseteste's essay on the "physics" of light.[10]

Thus also Pound's fine penetration of Dante? (I am thinking of those images of light in—and images of Beatrice, too—in the "Paradiso," is it, or is it at the end of the "Purgatorio"? Anyway, those which Eliot has made such a poor use of.)[11]

Maybe now I can get at this business of *amor* as of Ezra, and get at it right. It isn't a lack of the amorous, perhaps, so much as it is a completely different sense of the amorous to that which post-Christian man contains, to that which—to be most innocent about it, and properly relative—the likes of Duncan, say, or myself may feel.

(Of the likes of Bill W.? I am struck by the image of "fire" in "Paterson." Maybe fire is the opposite principle to light, and comes to the use of those who do not go the way of light. Fire has to consume to give off its light. But light gets its knowledge—and has its intelligence and its being—by going over things without the necessity of eating the substance of things in the process of purchasing its truth. Maybe this is the difference, the different base of not just these two poets, Bill and E. P., but something more, two contrary conceptions of love. Anyway, in the present context, it serves to characterize two differing personal *via*: one achieves its clarities by way of *claritas*, the other goes about its business blind, achieves its clarities by way of what you might call *confusio*. At which point I quote Chaucer's Cock to his Dame in the middle of the night on their perch. And quit the whole subject.

> For al so siker as *In principio*,
> *Mulier est hominis confusio*,—
> Madame, the sentence of this Latyn is,
> 'Womman is mannes joye and al his blis.'[12]

4

A long time ago (what, 25 years?) Pound took the role of Confucius, put on that mask, for good. I'm sure he would rest his claim not, as I have put it, on the past, but forward, as teacher of history to come, Culture-Bearer in the desert and shame of now. (I don't think it is possible to exaggerate the distance he goes with his notion of himself—at the end Gate of the last Canto Confucious is to be one of the two huge figures standing there, looking on.)[13]

It is all tied up with what he calls a truism, London, 1913: are you or are you not, a serious character?[14] Then it was Gaudier, Lewis and himself. Now it is the Major (Douglas), Lewis and himself. He sd that the other day, when we were talking about Bill Williams. Bill had just been taken to the hospital, and one of the new candidates on 2nd Avenue had had a letter from Bill repeating over and over again, "I have nothing to say, nothing to say." E. P. didn't pay this much mind. Sd he: "Bill has always been confused. He's one of the reasons I make so much of race. It's hard enough for a man to get things clear when he's of one race, but to be Bill!— french, spanish, anglo, some jew from Saragossa. . . ." And though I left Pound that day and shall not see him again, he went on to say something which is true, that what has made Bill important is that Bill has never sd one god damned thing that hasn't first circulated entirely through his head before it comes out his mouth. (Bill never faked, and that's why he has been of such use to all us young men who grew up after him. There he was in Rutherford to be gone to, and seen, a clean animal, the only one we had on the ground, right here in the States.)[15]

5

Pound makes a lot of the head. You can tell that he thinks of it as a pod, and most of the time comes to the conclusion that very little rattles around inside most known pods. The Major, Lewis and himself. The Major, Lewis and E. P. "Lewis," says he once, "Lewis most always gets things wrong. But he gets somethin'!"

At that point his wife got the conversation off on Eliot, and Hulme, confusing 1914 with 1913. Pound did not say that Eliot was not a serious character, what I gathered was that Pound had hoped the Possum might turn out to be one, in 1914. He then went on: "The war got Hulme too young. He used to spend three hours a week with the Bloomsbury gang, Ashley Dukes . ." he reeled off others "and we'd laugh at him, Gaudier, Lewis, I" and you could see Pound giving it to him. "But when he was gone, when he wasn't there to do it, we caught on, we saw what he'd been up to—he'd been beating that gang over the head hard enough every time he saw them to keep 'em in line. After he was gone, they went on the loose, there was no one to tell 'em . . . And look! . . ." Grampaw was giving a lesson.

Another lesson that day was his story of (Hunecker? no, some H, some citizen whose name I missed (they come flyin'), who was listening to Sturge Moore do a lecture,[16] or a reading, in one of those rooms which are built like an operating room, the seats steep and down like a bowl, and who was wishing that Moore would get on with it, and done, and holding his head in his hand, when a character in the row above him taps him on the shoulder, and sez, "Friend, don't feel so bad, what makes you think we're here to enjoy ourselves?"

He is driven, E. P., to get on with things, his things, the "serious." He sd to me another time: "I can't git it into yr american heads that the earth makes one complete circuit once EVERY 24 hrs."

Another crack: "I thought you might be a serious character when I read that labor-saving device of yrs on H. Melville. But that was 2 yrs ago, bro."[17]

6

When I happened to ask him what Frobenius looked like, I stumbled on the fact that Pound sees himself as a cat man. Both he and the wife quickened to the question. Glances were exchanged. He took it up, first: Sd he, "There were three men"—it was almost as though he said, once upon a time— "there were three men who might have come from the same genes. Frobenius . . ." DP interrupted, and started to go on to illustrate the differences between EP's face and Frobenius'. Then Pound was up on his feet, showing how F stood, back on his heels (P himself seems always on his toes, or did, before he thickened up from lack of exercise his second yr at SLiz, around the belly and below the back) with his arms out and his hands stuck in his belt, "He must 'ave got it from Africa," sez Pound (from the exigencies of the place, I judged, but the point being, all around the three of us, that E. P. never in his life would have spent the years that Frobenius did pushing around Africa). DP went on making with her hands, seeking further to show the differences—F not so wide at the temples . . . a V for F's beard, when all of a sudden old Ez lets it out, sort of half to her, all to me, "cat family, cat family," making with his head, and getting that fix in his oye![18]

And the 3rd of the same genes? "Barkoff, Barkoff" (EP with obvious delight) "now Chief of protocol, Moscow. (Pound had mentioned this Barkoff (Barkov, I suppose) several times two years earlier, particularly at the time when he was riding the idea that the U.S. Govt. could have saved itself a lot of trouble—and the world a lot of war—if it had allowed Old Ez what he asked for, the chance to pick up Georgian—"a week, 10 days"—and get over there and talk it out straight with Joe, in his own tongue. I gathered then that what would have made it all so simple was Barkov's presence, to rig the talk, once the USG wised up. Pound seems to have known Barkov years before, in Italy, perhaps, I don't know.)

7

Madame and Sir Pound also managed to get this across one day, that they had recently learned, "through Agnes,"[19] whoever she was, that Frobenius had said of E. P. before he died, "He is worth three Oxfords with four Cambridges on top."[20]

And it felt good to hear it, for these praises are old Ez's OM's and Nobel Awards. Joyce, apparently, was not a man to give praise out easily, and Pound told me once, with what pleasure, the only thing he ever got out of Joyce, this comment one day when he had read something new, "The sleek head of verse, Mr Pound, emerges in your work."[21]

He has a story of Joyce and Hauptmann, Joyce, when young, had translated one of Hauptmann's plays.[22] After Pound had met Hauptmann, Joyce put a copy of the play into Ezra's hands and asked him to get Hauptmann to autograph it for him. "And," says Ez, "he didn't write off one of those inscriptions"—the intervals, that way Pound gets gesture in between the letters even, showed that he was thinking of the way he does it, dashes them off—"he took it away, came back three days later, gave it to me, it read, to JJ the best reader this play ever had, and I shipped it off." At which point he cries out at the top of his delight, "He sure sat on that one till it hatched!"

8

Another of his comforts, is to see himself in the part of the Old Man, "Grandpa," now that Mary has made him one. Sd he the other day, mistaking, I think, the significance of what I was calling to his attention, the coming to Washington (as tho to Rome) of the "Poets" (Eliot at the National Gallery the spring before, which was like a laying on of hands, the coming into existence of an american poet laureate;[23] the creation, and the turnover, of the "poets of Congress," the Consultants; and, at the time I was speaking to him, the run of a series of readings at the new Institute of Contemporary Arts, Spender, Tate, Lowell & the other "Jrs"). Says the O.M.: "Ya, they'll all be coming to old Ez on his deathbed and telling him he was right"

and, when I was telling him about the way the people in the streetcars were shaking their heads like a bunch of dipping birds over a black new headline out of the Ant-Hill, "If they'd only listened to old Ez in the first place!"

"right,

right

from the start[24]

The American invasion of Europe—Invading Europe for 35 years had not ruined any historic monuments or art works, and destroyed no old mss. except my own.

* * *

Pound, as of 1939, great as Adams, Jefferson & Lincoln

* * *

Sewers of Freud & forests of Frobenius

* * *

Wyndham Lewis & Joyce rivals—out do each other drinking. One night they about killed each other. At any rate at the end of the night the two on curbstone with feet in gutter. J. to L. "You may paint this but I will write it."

Ford—Elsie captured him at 17 & thus he had no adolescence. 1911—passion for legality, & between his 1st & 2nd wife [was] at Giessen.[1] Ford Fordy drinking beer & eating ice cream, & having his undergraduate exp[erience].

At the same time, saved my literary career. Threw book & accused of not writing Anglese. So I had tried to write my third book in Oxfordese. F rolled on the floor, with his hands over his head, trying to teach me how to speak for myself.

London—1939—tried to get Communist & Fascists together

Sinology—tran.—if I can pull myself together. The trunk is down.

Lost 3 weeks—due to Dr ———— —you can't dig the root up —they've killed me.

Fordy—the Yid
The Kike Waley[2]
Eliot—the danger of his way——35 years of Criterion & never introduced a new writer in all that time[3]

* * *

Fixed fanaticism—Stalin. Save what's left of civilization. We can't be dominated by the Russians. Wife's uncle commander last war—Kipling poem on Russia[4]

Became interested in Muss from social credit. War between Italy & Am—anti-historic, crazy. They don't know what independence the Italians gave me.

Shaw's remark: If Christ came back now he'd be declared mentally unfit.

Freedom of speech

Greenbacks[5]—Social Credit—but don't know whether to mix up with it—Republicans are my best hope

* * *

the lag—I say, a hundred years

Fordie—to take the lice off Eliot's back. "He (E) took them off me." Cummings, Williams (to destroy Eliot) Stella says F selling again—He knew what was dangerous about Eliot from the start. In detached & broken sentences—Now I know the guck—maybe Fordie meant what he said—he did not understand me. He knew what was wrong, but he did not know what needed to be kept off the pages

Confucius—a man near 60 is no longer active, he can instruct younger men to action

Cagli—Zionist!—no more spreaders—incommunicado—must open line of communication. You are a culture. Eileen & you, nucleus of culture in Washington

form—of your book—additions in notes at bottom of page or appendix

* * *

It is time you met Lothrup Stoddard—I can't. He has had to
be low. Capitol Times—front page—1939—Tinkham let it go—
could have saved it with $10,000. Ask Stoddard what's happened
to the boys who were on it.[6]

It was the anti-semitism that got him. At the time of the Stock
break. (Mrs Stoddard has been to see Pound recently)

He was off on the Jewish business for fair. Gibberish about the
Old Testament being better than the new. He caught on when he
was doing the Cavalcanti. The Medieval boys went off when they
quoted the Old Testament. And He wasn't what the Jews wanted—
a bunch of nationalists and along comes this guy dishing out meta-
physics!

And about several Italians whose names I didn't recognize who
got in long ago, were civilized, and wanted to help stop the invasion
by Tartar ideas.

That's the line for Stoddard to follow—the Tartar thing. I told
Mosley (to lay off the anti-semitism?)[7]

Back on the Italian business, talking like a conspirator, muffling
everything so the guard wouldn't hear, & dropping into French. A lot
about Renenni (?)[8] who seemed to be Pound's boss or something—

Oh, yes, one interesting thing. The Italians weren't convinced
that Pound wasn't working for the U.S.!

It appears this Renenni went to see Ciano,[9] & C asked him
who have you got who is good, and when he said Pound, Ciano says,
"He's a Jew, isn't he?" At which R says: "Well, that is what they
say about you." At which Pound adds, like an old gossip, "You know,
his grandmother was a Jew—Jewess"

Somebody had told C to his face he was a s.o.b. I misunderstood & thot it was Pound himself. In answer he told the story of
the only time he ever saw him—at Princess Jane's. It seems C & Edda
were coming out as Pound came up in a cab. Edda had on a train
or a strip of her evening gown—a piece of satin abt the size, indicated Pound, of the large manila envelope I was carrying his Cantos

away in. It appears she had stepped on it & was giving C both barrels.

Musso—Olga (Mudge)[10]—"the loneliest creature I have ever seen"—after Matlesti[?]

Abt Italian politics: Olga: seeing the eye of the male which nails everything—she says: "All they want to do is fight each other, not foreigners"

The Axis was a mistake—I told Mosley—Italy natural friend of U.S.

* * *

Fenollosa[11]

—the Japs putting flowers on his grave

—the lack of interest of the Italian culture. Found these things unimportant

* * *

Briarcliffe—about Angold (best of the crop—pre-war—put an end to Rupert Brooke. EP was trans unpub prose into Italian when stopped[12]

Where each in his corner—where Cummings speaks only to Estlin & Estlin to no one at all

Santayana[13]—at least he's got to the point where he don't lie—he has no ethics—enlightened self-interest the closest

Binyon's trans[14]—fair, mild as he himself—a little dull—he said to me in 1907: "I can't do anything—quick" (pinched tone) "Slowness is beauty"

Frobenius is first—in communication: it isn't what a man says but what his hearer is ready to retain

* * *

Little magazines—by the three goyim—the one time the gang stayed together here. But I objected. Most of the time it all slid in

one [ear] and [out] the other—(as he said later, went soft)
Margaret Anderson published ½ without type, & threatened to issue
2nd all blank)[15]

America's been up Freud's asshole for 50 years

His eyes mean—on the ballot: "60 Monarch—40 but Russians
move in for Trieste"[16]

"the spoiled people of fascism the artisti"

MacLeish article—Sat Rev Lit.[17]

"My wife & Helen Weaver financed the 1st Prufrock.[18] Eliot
never knew it, doesn't now. It doesn't take much for creative work—
the thing is to have the little needed at the right moment—the right
time

"Dad & Possum"—Possum's slowness over O's education[19]

EP gave himself up to Am. authorities—he had important
information

It was a Lieut. Colonel who was responsible for Gorilla Cage

Howard B. Gill to find Corinthians Confucian! "I the 1st Confucian—I thot originally Legge knew the text, but he argued with
Confucius each time C did not fit St Paul."[20]

"Is there any question which is not answered in the text of the
4 books?"[21]

*   *   *

We mowed the grass for him (TSE), so he could set up his doll
house

They were 20 years behind time. That's why my first books
succeeded. I said so in Personae. Ford was the one contemporary &
he was ignored.

(Large, impersonal quality of EP today. The civilized man.
Not the ego)

His job on "Gabe" (in answer to Omar's question as to who
Gabriel d'Annunzio was)[22] The totality of his examination—even

to the retention of the attention to the simple thing, & his search to reach concision after the edition[?], & the astonishing image of the plaza, Venice, 1908 to the submarines 100 yds apart 1938

The victim is always culpable

If Muss. had gone to the university, no fascism

On the sounds of Chinese—versification—Euripedes—

If you men insist upon writing verse, go to the Greeks

I'm being educated from the spiel over teaching him (Omar). He's not getting a 10th as much. If you have a filing case this long —5 feet—you can get more in, [than on] a peck of paper in your pocket. That is one advantage in old age—

A propos my kafka-theory at Connie of last time, he asks C— "what I want to know is, is he vicious or provoked?"—I said the other day, to be in here before a man is 60, but there are 100,000,000 others outside.

Henry Crowder, Nancy Cunard's "coon,"[23] he and I the only civilized creatures in the whole place, and he the only "human value." Says Henry: Ah been readin' Mr Pound's Cantos. And Ah don know why I read em, cause I don' understand 'em. Snobbism, I guess.

Lewis & the dame the aviatrix who lost her life with Inchcliffe[24] —who could throw her silver mirror so accurately she caught Lewis on the back of the neck each time he passed out the doorway of her bedroom.

(His excitement over having the Book of Poetry ready—the ideogram, & its sound in Eng. & Japanese below it.)

Pound sounding the 4 vowels—not explosive but inplosive— pppahn.

His slash at the waste & vulgarity & then, magnificently, greatly "pour the wine on the altars" & the recompense (the ability to) focus the idea: thought the heart's field

His work to use Greek characters—on such things as war-chariots & sacrifice

The Spaniard 40 years ago who said: Thank God in my country a writer can not make a living by his pen. (a propos the dangers)

The past retained—Pound reaching his capacity & wondering how much he has retained—40 years

Another thing: Pound's insistence: study the Greek for versification, & leave the Greek vision alone—leave off the pagan business—not the Hellenic—H.D. did it[25]

* * *

Pound got on tail of Brooks Adams only in 1937–8, through John Slocum.[26]

Why do you think I've not quarreled with Eliot for 30 years, put up with him? One of the rarest among the goyim

About the ethnological business, "Olson, I have as much or more of a quarrel with the Swedes & the Irish as with the Yids—so you better watch out"

Eliot antagonism toward Cummings. A lot is due to The Dial, when he thought Cummings had too much to do with it

On HLM,[27] he swung off on some business of, if 2 people see the same object the same, it is either symmetrical or one of them is a liar (Very good)

Hard if you think I should have the same opinions at 60 I had at 20—

"If I had read Old Wives Tale at the time I knew Bennett I should certainly have cremated him."[28]

A propos my report on the age of Eliot at the Church house. Says Pound, "Why do you think I baptized him? (Possum) CO "I don't know—does a possum smell under his tail?" EP "The possum: ability to appear to be dead while it is still alive"

Wyndham Lewis—on Eliot: 1½ hr every two repeating himself. Provocation, tho—Eliot's review of TAR[29]

The sense of Pound's struggle to keep his head above things, against the others, Eliot, Joyce, Lewis, Yeats even. Especially the value he put on Joyce's praise—then my reminder of J's words abt [what he] owe[d] to Pound on language.[30] Then P on his "sleek head of verse."

* * *

(These are Olson's final words on Pound. They were written four weeks before Olson's death.—Ed.)

I am astonished actually that Ezra shld have had any particular knowledge (other than rubbed off from Yeats') of Rabindranath Tagore.[31]

Which only shows my ignorance as you'd hardly have the subject.

From my own side (of the pickle) I can say I hardly think Tagore wld have been much EPs dish. And at least I can give you back (for your inquiry) a story of Ezra's (in another context) which I *very* much suspect must have been somewhere when he could have [been] playing along on the Tagore flute: he told me once in St. Elizabeths (early, when I was visiting him when he was still in Howard Hall, the Federal pen proper) that Yeats used to pester him so much when the Yeatses wld visit Rapallo hoping and asking Ezra to be a 4th at table-rapping!

(Which Ezra wld tell with exact American impatience at the time wasted, and equally with his own marked & particular graciousness, that I'm sure he often gave in.

Charles Olson

Regards, and of course (in addition to my not knowing anything abt the Tagore attention) I equally am and always [have] been impressed by his searing lumping of Hindooism & Hebraism in that slashing attack upon Greekism as well, in the essay called "Medievalism" (is it not?) in the Cavalcanti essays?[32]

Regards—& excuses for the handwriting. I am getting it off to you as soon as possible from a hospital bed! Friday December 5, 1969

Preface

1. Letter from Olson to Cid Corman [March 24, 1951] in Charles Olson, *Letters for Origin, 1950–1956,* ed. Albert Glover (New York, 1970), p. 40.
2. In Olson's notebook for Fall 1945, in a rather extensive critical dialogue with himself on the subject of his prose, he writes: "Hunch each step of the way. You have rid yourself of the orphic, a little. Continue to beat with the hammer to get the proper sculpture."
3. Letter from Olson to Cid Corman, November 25, 1950, in Olson, *Letters for Origin,* p. 20.

Introduction

1. From a letter of Pound's in Julien Cornell, *The Trial of Ezra Pound* (New York, 1966), p. 71.
2. Edward Dahlberg inscribed "Woman" in *Can These Bones Live* (Norfolk, Conn., 1960), to Olson: ". . . How much of our talks have yeasted and bloomed this little Herman Melville loaf; and how I have played the cutpurse Autolycus, making my thefts as invisible as possible, you and my blushes best know. But here is my hand with Mephistopheles' orison: When your own polestar Truths surge upon the whited page, may 'God's spies' put the same vermilion Guilt upon your face!"
3. *Charles Olson Reading at Berkeley* ([Berkeley], 1966), p. 32.
4. Copy of a letter to Pound from Olson enclosed in a letter to Robert Creeley from Olson, June 19, 1950.
5. *Olson Reading at Berkeley,* p. 28.
6. "The Art of Poetry XII: Charles Olson," *Paris Review,* Summer 1970, pp. 181–82.

7. Frank Ledlie Moore, a young composer and close friend of Olson's during this period. Moore was an early and consistent visitor of Pound's at St. Elizabeths and spent some time with Pound at Brunnenburg Castle (Pound's daughter's home) working on a score for Pound's *Women of Trachis.*

8. *Olson Reading at Berkeley,* p. 13. Lewis C. Frank, Jr., was a colleague of Olson's at OWI. He was public relations director of the National Citizens Political Action Committee in the 1944 Presidential campaign, on Wallace's staff of *The New Republic* and later Wallace's aide and speechwriter during the 1948 campaign.

9. *Survey Graphic* 33, no. 8 (August 1944) : 356.

10. From Pound's broadcast of July 22, 1942, printed in Charles Norman, *The Case of Ezra Pound* (New York, 1968), p. 53.

11. Pound, *ABC of Economics* (London, 1933), p. 119.

12. Olson, *Call Me Ishmael* (New York, 1947), p. 21.

13. Major Clifford Hugh Douglas (1879–1952), a Scot social economist who introduced the theory of social credit that Pound championed.

14. *Letters for Origin,* p. 35. For Olson on economics in 1964, see "A Bibliography for Ed Dorn," *Additional Prose* . . . (Bolinas, Calif., 1974), p. 14.

15. "The Art of Poetry XII" p. 198.

16. John Finch, Olson's roommate at Wesleyan University, now professor of drama, Dartmouth College. Melville was Olson's first great literary love. Edward Dahlberg, a close friend of Olson's during the late 1930s and early 1940s, whom Olson called his "other man of Cross and Windmills" in an unused dedicatory phrase intended for *Call Me Ishmael.* Corrado Cagli, Italian painter in America from 1938 to 1948. Cagli and Olson collaborated on *Y&X,* Olson's first book of poems, published in 1948 by the Black Sun Press.

    By 1969 Olson had revised his list of fathers: his real father; Wilbert Snow, friend and professor of English at Wesleyan; Lou Douglas, a Gloucester fisherman; Carl Sauer, professor of geography, University of California, whom Olson met during his West Coast trip in 1947; and Pound, the only surviving name from the original list. Charles Boer, *Charles Olson in Connecticut* (Chicago, 1975).

17. *Olson Reading at Berkeley,* p. 30.

18. Letter to Catherine Seelye from Dr. Jerome Kavka, August 21, 1973.

19. Michael Reck, *Ezra Pound, A Close-Up* (London, 1968), p. 86.

20. Olson was having problems during this same period with his feelings about his own father, long since dead. This struggle came to a head in *The Post Office* [written in early 1948] (Bolinas, Calif., 1975).

21. John Kasper and T. David Horton, two of Pound's frequent and continuing visitors at St. Elizabeths, both far to the right in their politics, were the publishers of the Square Dollar Series, inspired and at least partly directed by Pound. (For more on the Square Dollar Series, see Noel Stock, *The Life of Ezra Pound* [New York, 1970] pp. 430–32.) Kasper's involvement in the white supremacy movement in the South in the 1950s is often cited as having been a deterrent to efforts to gain Pound's early release.
22. Olson, *Causal Mythology* (San Francisco, 1969), p. 2.
23. Ibid., pp. 13–14.

A Lustrum for You, E. P.

Editor's note: Olson is referring to Mathew Brady's photograph *At the Hanging.* See Roy Meredith, *Mr. Lincoln's Camera Man* (New York, 1946), plate 120. Pound's "*ABCs*" are his *ABC of Economics and ABC of Reading.* "Sligo Willie" is William Butler Yeats, who spent much of his youth in County Sligo (Ireland) with his grandparents. Olson was aware that it was not Yeats but Wyndham Lewis who coined the epitaph "Revolutionary Simpleton." Yeats, in a letter to Lady Gregory, had quoted Lewis, who first applied the phrase to Pound in his review, *The Enemy*, January 1927, and repeated it in *Time and Western Man* and in several later books. Propertius is one of Pound's personae (see his poem "Homage to Sextus Propertius"). Olson refers on several occasions to Pound as "Montana." The myth of Montana may have started with a notice of Pound's *Personae* in *Punch*, June 23, 1909, in which Pound is referred to as the "new Montana (U.S.A.) poet." Ford Madox Ford perpetuates the myth in *Return to Yesterday*: "though born in Butte." Pound himself may have added to the confusion by his stating in *Indiscretions* that his grandmother and her mother lived in Montana. And finally, how can a poet write "Listen, Idaho" when he has the option of writing "Listen, Montana"? Olson incorporates into this poem several passages from Pound's *Jefferson and/or Mussolini* and at least one quotation from *The Cantos* ("19 years on that case/first case"). And Pound's remark "if a man isn't willing to take some risk" is from Charles Norman's article, "The Case For and Against Ezra Pound," *PM*, November 25, 1945.

Your Witness

Editor's note: This poem consists of quotations from Pound—two from *The Cantos* ("another war without glory, another peace without quiet"— Canto XXI; "19 years on this case/first case. I have set down part of"— Canto XLVI); two viva voce ("Well, if I ain't worth more alive than dead. . ." and "If a man isn't willing to take some risk . . . ," reported by Charles Norman in *PM*, November 25, 1945; and the remainder from *Jefferson and/or Mussolini*. A few quotations were altered by Olson. For example, Pound writes in *Jefferson and/or Mussolini*, "Journalism as I see it is history of to-day, and literature is journalism that stays news." Olson writes, "journalist. As I see it history of today / literature is that stays news."

Fragments

1. "I may . . . find . . . that seemingly irrelevant details fit together into a single theme, that here is no botch of tone and colour—Hodos Chamelion-tos—except for some odd corner where one discovers beautiful detail. . . ." William Butler Yeats, *A Packet for Ezra Pound* (Dublin, 1929), pp. 3–4.
2. Jane Anderson and Frederick Wilhelm Kaltenbach were two of eight persons (including Pound) who were indicted by the U.S. government in July 1943 for broadcasting Axis propaganda. Charges were dropped against Anderson in 1947 for insufficient evidence. Charges were dropped against Kaltenbach in 1948 when Russia notified the United States that Kaltenbach had died in 1945 in a Russian concentration camp.
3. "Why should anyone starve? That is the crude and rhetorical question. It is as much our question as Hamlet's melancholy was the problem of the renaissance dyspeptic." Pound, *ABC of Economics* (London, 1933), p. 18.
4. Rudolf Hess, Third Deputy in Hitler's cabinet, sentenced to life imprisonment at Nürnberg.
5. Hermann Göring, Nazi economic minister and commander of the Luftwaffe. Sentenced to death at Nürnberg. Göring committed suicide. Julius Streicher, Nazi proponent of annihilation of all Jews. Sentenced to death at Nürnberg.

This Is Yeats Speaking

1. From Yeats's "All Souls' Night: Epilogue to 'A Vision.'"

First Canto

1. Bolitha J. Laws, Chief Justice of the District Court for the District of Columbia.
2. Julien Cornell. See his *The Trial of Ezra Pound; A Documented Account of the Treason Case* . . . (London, 1967).
3. "At the elevator, as Pound left the court building, Cornell . . . said 'maybe you'd like to read the paper while you're lying down,' and handed him a folded newspaper. Pound looked at it and tossed it back to Cornell. 'I don't read the New York *Times*,' he snapped." Charles A. Michie, "Pound a Sad Spectacle at Bar," *PM*, November 28, 1945.
4. Mary de Rachewiltz, daughter of Ezra Pound and Olga Rudge. Omar Pound, son of Ezra and Dorothy Pound.
5. Gallinger Hospital, Washington, D.C., to which Pound was moved November 27, 1945, from the Washington Asylum and Jail. Pound remained at Gallinger until December 21, 1945, when he was transferred to St. Elizabeths Hospital for the Insane.
6. A clipping in Olson's "Pound file" from an unidentified newspaper reports: "French Supply Minister Bonnet told of flying from Paris to Washington in a plane in which the poet–treason defendant Ezra Pound was also a passenger. Bonnet said that Pound, in dirty shirt and soiled prison clothes, sat silent and bored for hours, until the sun began to shine. Suddenly Pound sprang up and, looking down at the tremendous sunlit sea, became, on his first ocean crossing by air, ecstatic, like a bird let out of a cage, like a man pulled out of a deep, dark hole. He paced the aisle declaiming in poetic rhapsody."
7. Edmund Ziman and Jerome Kavka, psychiatrists on the staff of St. Elizabeths Hospital.
8. *Confucius: The Unwobbling Pivot and the Great Digest* (Norfolk, Conn., 1947).
9. Not yet identified.
10. Pound may have said "Chew" as he did in Canto XXII: "Yais, he ees a goot fello, / But after all a chew / ees a chew."

11. Howard Hall was a section of St. Elizabeths Hospital where all federal prisoners under indictment were confined. Pound was kept in Howard Hall until February 4, 1947, when he was transferred to Chestnut Ward, a less restricted section of the hospital. Pound remained in Chestnut Ward until his release from confinement in 1958.
12. The steel cage in which Pound was detained for several weeks while at the American Disciplinary Training Center near Pisa.
13. Pound was in the custody of the Counter Intelligence Center, Genoa, from May 3, 1945, to May 24, 1945, when he was turned over to the authorities at Pisa where he was imprisoned for six months.
14. Warren Gamaliel Harding.
15. Alessandro Pavolini, Minister of Popular Culture, 1940–1943? Pavolini received his appointment through the intervention of his friend Conte Ciano, Mussolini's son-in-law and well-known critic of Mussolini's war policies (see also note 9 to the Appendix).
16. Klaus Mann, author, son of Thomas Mann.
17. Ida and Adah Lee Mapel, two sisters from Georgetown whom Pound had met in Spain in 1906. The Mapels, according to Eustace Mullins in *This Difficult Individual, Ezra Pound*, were the "originals of the 'Soeurs Randall' of the *Imaginary Letters*." They may well have been also the Americans whom Pound showed around Spain in 1906 with the help of a Baedeker.
18. *Guide to Kulchur* was first published by Faber & Faber in 1938. It was issued the same year in America by New Directions under the title *Culture*. For a discussion of changes made by the publisher, see Noel Stock, *The Life of Ezra Pound* (New York, 1970), p. 354.

Canto 2

1. Caresse Crosby (1892–1970) was founder (with Harry Crosby), editor, and publisher of the Black Sun Press. She published Pound's *Imaginary Letters* in 1930 and Olson's first book of poems, *Y&X*, in 1948.
2. George Holden Tinkham (1870–1956), Republican representative from Massachusetts, 1915–1943. Tinkham was noted for his isolationist views, his insistence on separation of church and state, his opposition to prohibition, and, of special interest to Pound, his belief that international bankers and business men were influencing the foreign policy of the United States.

3. Westbrook Pegler, a right-wing columnist for Scripps-Howard and Hearst newspapers.

4. Probably a piece called "Remember Ezra?" (*Newsweek*, December 3, 1945, pp. 38–39) in which Pound was referred to as America's Lord Haw Haw.

5. Among the many charges brought against Pound by the U.S. government was Pound's acceptance of "payment and remuneration . . . from the Kingdom of Italy for compiling and recording messages, speeches and talks for subsequent broadcasts." Pound claimed that the compensation was barely sufficient to cover the costs incurred by his travel between Rome and Rapallo.

6. Pound had written to the *Boston Herald* (February 7, 1939) that Tinkham would make a good President and that Massachusetts should send him to the White House. And in the same year in an interview with a reporter from the Utica *Observer-Dispatch*, Pound said, "If God loved the American people the Republican Party would nominate for President George Holden Tinkham."

7. Tinkham's "letters to the Treasury" have not been identified.

8. Olson felt his father had been harassed to death (he died of a stroke in 1935) by the U.S. Post Office in retribution for his earlier efforts to gain benefits for the National Association of Letter Carriers, of which he was a member.

9. Henri Gaudier-Brzeska (1891–1915), French sculptor whom Pound met in London in 1913. Much of Gaudier's fame and success is due to Pound's championing of him. Gaudier's early death in World War I affected Pound deeply, and he memorialized him in *Gaudier-Brzeska: A Memoir* . . . in 1916.

10. *View*, published in New York from 1940 to 1945/46, was a little magazine devoted primarily to surrealism in literature and art on an international level.

11. "London stank of decay back before 1914 and I have recorded the feel of it in a poem here and there. The live man in a modern city feels this sort of thing or perceives it as the savage perceives in the forest." *Jefferson and/or Mussolini: L'Idea Statale; Fascism as I Have Seen It* (New York, [1936]), pp. 48–49.

12. Possibly Levi Berman with whom Olson worked in New York and Washington.

13. *Imaginary Letters* (Paris, 1930).

14. Pound discontinued his broadcasts for almost two months after Pearl Harbor.

15. Olson's friend Michael Greenberg, who was one of Roosevelt's advisers on Far Eastern policy.
16. "If I ain't worth more alive than dead, that's that. If a man isn't willing to take some risk for his opinions, either his opinions are no good or he's no good." Charles Norman, "The Case For and Against Ezra Pound," *PM*, November 25, 1945.
17. Ernest Poole (1880–1950).
18. In a letter to A. S. Elwell Sutton (quoted by Noel Stock, *The Life of Ezra Pound* [New York, 1970], p. 327), Pound quotes Yeats on this point and goes on to say, "Which he elaborated: certain opinions get whispered around as the 'right thing.'"
19. John Boynton Priestley, English novelist, critic, playwright, and immensely popular radio commentator during World War II.
20. The outburst reported by Pound was brought on by "Van Dine, a long Hollander who had drifted into Chicago a bit before 1917, and had applied for American citizenship; he got a tax form, describing him as an alien, subject to certain imposts, and he got called up for army service. He said to the judge: 'I am perfectly willing to serve in the army, but if I am citizen enough to serve in the army I've got a right not to be taxed as a foreigner.'" *Jefferson and/or Mussolini*, p. 97.
21. The Mapel sisters.
22. *Savage Messiah* (New York, 1931) was written by Harold Stanley Ede. Mary's uncle Ted was Olga Rudge's brother, Edward, who lived in London.
23. Mary Butts (1893–1937) was a surrealist writer whom Pound met in Paris. Ronald Duncan was a poet and playwright and editor of the *Townsman*, to which Pound frequently contributed. Neither *The Death of Felicity Taverner* nor *Journal of a Husbandman* was published by New Directions. Olson read Duncan's *Husbandman* "with deep satisfaction." He wrote a review of it for *Tomorrow* and submitted it to Pound for his comments. Pound made kind but devastating notes on the copy and it was never published.
24. Austine Cassini was a columnist for the Washington, D.C., *Times-Herald*. The article referred to by Pound was probably the column "These Charming People," which appeared in the *Times-Herald* on December 11, 1945, in which Mrs. Cassini quotes from "The Tomb of Akr Caar": "And no sun comes to rest me in this place, / And I am torn against the jagged dark, / And no light beats upon me, and you say / No word, day after day. / Oh! I could get me out, despite the marks / And all their crafty

work upon the door, / Out through the glass-green fields. . . . / Yet it is quiet here: / I do not go." She goes on to list the poets "who have come to grief in their own countries" and asks, "Is it that poets are perfectionists, always dissatisfied with the state of the world and, misguided though they be, forever battling futilely and frantically to transform and better imperfect politics, places and people?"

25. John O'Donnell's remarks on Pound appeared in his column, "Capitol Stuff," in the Washington *Times-Herald*. On November 27, 1945, O'Donnell reported on Pound's indictment and quoted a portion of one of Pound's broadcasts along with Pound's defense of his broadcasting activities. On November 28, O'Donnell described the "Pound jail library": an English translation of *Confucius, The Handbook of Verse*, and so forth. And on December 3, O'Donnell apologized for stating that Pound was born in Iowa.

Canto 3

1. Constance Wilcock Bunker, Olson's first wife.
2. Bertram's is a tobacco shop in Washington.
3. "Do not be elected to the Senate of your country. I think myself, after six years, well out of that of mine. Neither you nor I, nor any other of our excitable profession, can match these old lawyers, old bankers, old business men, who, because all habit and memory, have begun to govern the world." William Butler Yeats, *A Packet for Ezra Pound* (Dublin, 1929), p. 33.
4. Pound attended Hamilton College and the University of Pennsylvania.
5. *Jefferson and/or Mussolini: L'Idea Statale; Fascism as I Have Seen It* (London, 1935; New York, [1936]).
6. Francis Biddle, U.S. Attorney General, 1941–1945, who handed down Pound's indictment in 1943.
7. Dr. Jerome Kavka does not recall any particular reference to Poland by Pound except in reference to Kavka's Polish origins on those occasions when Pound felt a need to strike back at his questioner. Kavka does believe that Pound's bitterness over the outbreak of World War I in 1914 and the resulting deaths of Gaudier and Hulme had much to do with his later problems. (Conversation between Dr. Kavka and Catherine Seelye, December 28, 1973.)
8. Count Jerzy Potocki (1889–1961), Polish ambassador to the United

States, 1936–1940. Pound lunched with Potocki while in Washington in 1939.

9. Max Brod, in *Franz Kafka; Eine Biographie*, points out that Kavka is the correct spelling of this name.

10. Dr. Edmund Ziman "was called Tiny because he was a very portly man resembling to some extent one of his close personal friends, Zero Mostel. He had a great sense of humor and was most articulate." Letter to Catherine Seelye from Dr. Jerome Kavka, August 21, 1973.

11. Olson invited Kavka to dinner on January 4, 1946 (the day of Olson's first visit to Pound). Kavka declined "for fear of compromising the case." Ibid.

12. Dr. Edgar D. Griffin, Clinical Director of Clinical Branch II, St. Elizabeths Hospital.

13. DTC. Disciplinary Training Center, Mediterranean Theater of Operations USA, near Pisa.

14. Ibid.

15. Philip Rahv, editor of *The Partisan Review*, accepted Olson's "This Is Yeats Speaking."

16. Probably Olson's friend Oscar Lange (1904–1965), a Pole by birth, one time professor of economics, University of Chicago, who renounced his naturalized U.S. citizenship in 1945 to become Poland's ambassador to the United Nations. Olson met Lange through Adam Kulikowski, a consultant to the OWI.

17. Olson wrote Donald Allen of Grove Press in April 1958: "Publishing coup of present (now that Pound's out of hospital and indictment dismissed) is the *full* transcript of his *broadcasts*—without alleviation or explanations. Document #1 of American *literary* Republic. Cannot urge on you, and thru you on Barney [Rosset], anything equal to it text-wise for our times."

18. *Some Do Not*, published in 1924, followed by *No More Parades* in 1925, the first two volumes of the "Tietjens Tetralogy."

Canto 4

1. U.S. Justice Department files indicate that this was Dr. Marion R. King, who was Medical Director for the Bureau of Prisons in 1946 and one of the four psychiatrists who examined Pound.

2. Probably to the pilgrimage-church, Madonna di Montallegro, which is situated some two thousand feet above Rapallo.

3. V. N. Barkov, head of the Protocol Department, People's Commissariat of Foreign Affairs, USSR, 1931–1939.
4. Leo Frobenius (1873–1938), German ethnologist and explorer, founder of the Forschungsinstitut für Kulturmorphologie. Frobenius is known to the world at large primarily due to Pound's interest in him.
5. Hugh Dalton (1887–1962), English social economist and member of the Labour party, was Chancellor of the Exchequer from 1945 until his resignation in 1947.
6. Olson's reference eludes me. He may have been referring to one of the many rumors concerning Clement Attlee's appointments after the victory of the Labour party in July 1945. Dalton discusses in detail these appointments and their attendant rumors in his *Memoirs*, but he does not mention a stand taken by him and Sir Stafford Cripps against Ernest Bevin in favor of a "Dalton man." Cripps had aligned himself immediately after the election with Herbert Morrison, who wanted the leadership, in an effort to forestall the formation of a government by Attlee until the party could "elect" a leader, but both Dalton and Bevin stood behind Attlee.
7. American dollars.
8. Henry Tudor Tucker, brother of Olivia Shakespear, Pound's mother-in-law.
9. For a discussion of Major Douglas and his "A + B" theory, see John L. Finlay, *Social Credit: The English Origins* (Montreal, 1972). It was largely through Douglas's articles in Alfred R. Orage's *The New Age* that Pound became an ardent advocate of social credit. Although he did not embrace with equal enthusiasm all its aspects, Pound believed the scheme would work. He was irresistibly drawn to it as he saw a means whereby banks could be controlled by the government (read community), and their credit-making powers curtailed, whereby the value of money would be stabilized, and whereby the value of work done would be justly compensated. As a Jeffersonian-Confucian-elitist, Pound believed in a "conspiracy of intelligent men": the "West End" must be preserved "to set a model for living." And he felt this would be guaranteed by Douglas's scheme, which was based on an "aristocratic hierarchy of producers" serving a "democracy of consumers," while at the same time assuring a more equitable sharing of the fruits of labor. (Pound also found his views of the "Jewish problem" in concert with those of Douglas: both were opposed to the "power-seeking conspiracy" of Jews, but both liked and respected individual Jews.)
10. "The Mahometans ran on a share-out system. I forgot whether every

fanatic got an equal share. It don't much matter, it was so long ago, but at any rate they had national dividends, at least as long as they continued to conquest." Ezra Pound, *ABC of Economics* (London, 1933), p. 81.

11. Silvio Gesell (1862–1930). Pound is referring to Gesell's theory of "stamped" money: money kept in circulation was not taxed; money saved (hoarded) was taxed. Taxing would be in the form of stamps purchased each month and fixed to the currency. It has been suggested that Pound's fondness for stamp scrip stemmed from his love of gadgets. He was certainly aware of the use to which scrip could be put in lieu of money by the example of his grandfather who issued scrip when his lumber company was in tight financial straits. He told Olson that his grandfather had the "same economic ideas that I am struggling for." Pound saw in stamp scrip a way to keep money in circulation which would force economic activity, and a way to provide for the sharing of the common wealth through low-rate interest. His ultimate aim was to curb the power of private banks, to return the control of money (i.e., credit) to the government (i.e., the people), and to equate purchasing power with production in order to insure a minimum standard of living. He saw in both the Douglas and Gesell schemes ways to gain these ends and refused to admit they were incompatible. He proposed, for example, that national dividends (if they must be paid) be paid in stamps.

12. Pound was reluctant to accept Douglas's plan to pay national dividends, a proposal which smacked of social equality. Pound believed in work, but he insisted that it be justly compensated. He claimed, in an effort to reassure dissenters from social credit who were disenchanted with its "antiwork" complexion, that the dividends would be paid only to those who agreed to work. Finlay, *Social Credit*, p. 213. But he knew this was not the case and admitted at one point that "the turbine can work for the group . . . the idea of national dividends (which I dislike) seems less goofy from this angle." Pound, *ABC of Economics*, p. 101.

13. Although Gesell was not a socialist, he was chosen as Finanzminister of Bavaria in the Lindhauer government in April 1919 because of his knowledge of money and economic systems. His *Die natürliche Wirtschaftsordnung durch Freiland und Freigeld* was then in its third edition. Gesell was intrigued by the opportunity to try out his monetary theories, but he was unable to do so as he was in office only a few days when the government was overthrown. For a life of Gesell, see Werner Schmid, *Silvio Gesell: die Lebensgeschichte eines Pioniers* (Bern, 1954).

14. Edmondo Rossoni, Italian Minister of Agriculture and Forests, 1935–1940. Rossoni was a revolutionary labor agitator in the United States in the years prior to World War I and later became the leader of the Fascist labor unions in the early years of the Italian Fascist state.

15. *Eleven New Cantos* was inscribed: "To Chas Olson / saviour / as it were / onlye sustainer / Ezra Pound / 46." The second inscribed volume has not been located.

16. "Pound was not drunk at any time that I spoke with him but actually was referring to an episode in his past life when he had too much. This he told me when I inquired as to his consumption of alcohol. My general impression is that he was nowhere near being a drinker of any volume." Letter to Catherine Seelye from Dr. Jerome Kavka, February 24, 1974.

17. The gestures, movement, and music can only be imagined. The words can be seen in *An "Objectivists" Anthology*, ed. by Louis Zukofsky ([Le Beausset, France], 1932), pp. 44–45. In "I, Mencius, Pupil of the Master . . . ," Olson refers to this dance of Pound's: "(Old Bones / do not try to dance / go still / now that your legs / the Charleston / is still for us / You can watch."

18. Harry Meacham in *The Caged Panther* (New York, 1967), p. 24, reports that Pound learned of the indictment from "*Time* or some other news source." Noel Stock (*The Life of Ezra Pound* [New York, 1970], p. 397) gives, as one account, the BBC. For a text of Pound's letter to Attorney General Biddle, see Charles Norman, *The Case of Ezra Pound* (New York, 1968), pp. 63–65.

Canto 5

1. The four psychiatrists who were appointed by the court to judge Pound's competency to stand trial: Joseph L. Gilbert, Marion R. King, Wendell Muncie, and Winfred Overholzer.

2. The hearing was held February 13, 1946.

3. Dr. Hugo R. Fack (whom Pound called a "country physician" in *Guide to Kulchur*) published from 1931 to 1950 a paper under the titles of (1) *Freedom and Plenty*, (2) *The Way Out*, and (3) *Free-Economy: The Way Out for Democracy*. Fack devoted his publishing activities to the espousal of Silvio Gesell and his theories, publishing Gesell's *The Natural Economic Order* and a series of pamphlets entitled the Neo-Economic

Series of Freedom and Plenty. *Freedom and Plenty* 16, no. 2 (February 1946), contained an article called, "Ezra Pound—Poet and Money Reformer: Traitor or Patriot?" in which Pound was quoted as saying, "If only Vinson knew Truman didn't think me an idiot." "Truman" should have read "Tremaine," probably Morris S. Tremaine, the highly respected Controller of the State of New York for many years.

4. See Pound's Canto XIII for the source of Olson's poem below.

A Translation

King Tching T'ang's inscription:
AXE TREE SUN

> The AXE to put away old habit

> New as the young grass shoot
> wrote Kung interpreting TREE

> look to a constant renovation LOOK to
> as each new day
> look: the sun!

on the bathtub:

AXE TREE SUN

5. Cantos LXXI and LXXII have not yet been published.
6. Probably Ambrogio Praedis. See Pound's Canto XLV.
7. Yeats's description of the cantos is found in his *A Packet for Ezra Pound* (Dublin, 1929), pp. 2–4.
8. *Portfolio: An Intercontinental Quarterly* (published in Washington, D.C., and Paris by the Black Sun Press, 1945–1948). Olson's poem "Upon a Moebus Strip" appeared in the Spring 1947 issue.
9. Giorgio di Chirico, Italian surrealist painter.
10. Cagli's murals decorating the lobby of the Italian Pavilion of the Paris Exposition of 1937 were partly destroyed when the exhibition was ordered closed by Ciano. Cagli left Italy in 1938 for Paris and then on to the United States, where he lived until 1948.
11. *Whistle Stop*, a novel of an American degenerate family, by Maritta Wolff, first published in 1941.
12. *Some Do Not* and *No More Parades*.
13. The canto on love is Canto XXXVI; the canto on Artemis is Canto XXX.

Canto 6

1. The version here differs from the published text, as Pound made changes on the proofs.
2. The "Gorilla cage" had a cement floor upon which Pound sat and slept. A cot was added later (along with a pup tent which Pound could erect to keep out the elements).
3. *Call Me Ishmael* was published by Reynal & Hitchcock the following year.
4. Olson sent the manuscript to Eliot, who rejected it as being too sophisticated a treatment of Melville for an English audience.
5. *This Way to the Tomb.* See Ronald Duncan's Introduction to his *Collected Plays* (New York, 1970) for a discussion of the forces which led Duncan to write the play and of Eliot's part in the writing of it.
6. "I take SPACE to be the central fact to man born in America, from Folsom cave to now."
7. Douglas Fox, Frobenius' American assistant and collaborator on *African Genesis* and *Prehistoric Rock Pictures in Europe and Africa.* Fox was alive at this time and in fact he and Olson shortly thereafter exchanged a few letters, Olson suggesting that Fox's *New English Weekly* articles be collected and republished and that Fox continue his translations of the Atlantis series.
8. There is no thirty-volume work of Frobenius of which I am aware. Pound may have been referring to Frobenius' total published output or perhaps to the publications of the Forschungsinstitut für Kulturmorphologie. Pound considered *Paideuma* (vol. 4 of *Erlebte Erdteile*) to be Frobenius' most important work and had planned to translate it in 1929 but could find no publisher for it. See Noel Stock, *The Life of Ezra Pound* (New York, 1970), p. 285.
9. Eugene Reynal of Reynal & Hitchcock.
10. F. V. Morley, a director of Faber & Faber.

Canto 7

1. *ABC of Economics* was first published in 1933; *Jefferson and/or Mussolini* was first published in 1935.
2. Not yet identified.

3. Serafima Astafieva (Eliot's "Grishkin") was a member of Diaghilev's ballet company and among the first of the Russians to open a school of ballet in London. She was a friend of Pound's, and he introduced Eliot to her. Pound reports the meeting in a letter to H. B. Parkes in 1931 (?) (see Donald Gallup, *T. S. Eliot & Ezra Pound* [New Haven, 1970] p. 11), and in "A Matter of Modesty," Pound writes, "ust like when I took Parson Elyot to see the Prima Ballerina and it evoked 'Grushkin'; as you can see in the bewteeful poEM entytled 'Whispers of Immortality.' " Years later, in Canto LXXVII, Pound writes: "or Grishkin's photo re-found years after /with the feeling that Mr Eliot may have / missed something, after all, in composing his vignette."

4. Olson's specific complaint, as he expressed it in a letter to Robert Creeley in 1950, was Eliot's "use of my, *my* madonna, buono viaggi, Gloucester, and how he misuses it, is riding, is generalizer."

5. "*The Old Wives' Tale* is one of the best artistic presentations of life in Paris that I have ever read." Ford Madox Ford, *Return to Yesterday* (New York, 1932), p. 183.

6. Arnold Bennett (1867–1931) was one of the most powerful reviewers in England, "a maker and breaker of reputations." Ford may have been referring to Bennett's advice, which appears in Pound's *Hugh Selwyn Mauberley*, to "butter reviewers."

7. Ford befriended Dahlberg and offered to act as his literary agent. Dahlberg writes that he had lost his "only defender, and after he was gone I was to be forgotten for many years." *The Confessions of Edward Dahlberg* (New York, 1971), p. 204. Dahlberg introduces his essays *Can These Bones Live* with a "lated tribute" to Ford: "As I deeply bow to place my lips upon your Brow, in gratitude for your Grace and dispensations to me, I weep because my homage is the coarse and pusillanimous thanks of the living to the dead. My pardon and my sorrow, Kind Genius, Good, Savory Ford Madox Ford." *Can These Bones Live* (Norfolk, Conn., 1960), p. 41. In 1965 Dahlberg is still remembering his debt to Ford: "A moribund 'old man mad about writing' . . . and hardly able to breathe he read my ms., *Can These Bones Live*, and offered to write the Introduction to it, but he died in Deauville." *The New York Review of Books*, September 30, 1965, p. 4.

8. *Moby Dick.*

9. William Ellery Sedgwick. "Harvard never granted 'young Ellery,' as we called him, tenure, and for his advance in professional rank he was I suppose in competition with Ted Spencer (whom Harvard passed over but later recalled). Spencer was the more ambitious and aggressive of

the two, and I think this is what Olson had in mind." Letter to Catherine Seelye from Edward Weeks, December 20, 1973.

10. Olson appeared with the Ballet Russe de Monte Carlo in Léonide Massine's production of *Bacchanale* in Boston in April 1940. Marc Platoff had a principal dancing role. For an account of this episode, see John Finch, "Dancer and Clerk," *The Massachusetts Review*, Winter 1971.

11. Hubert J. Stowitts (sometimes spelled Stowitz) met Pavlova while he was a student at the University of California. He became Pavlova's dancing partner, choreographer, and designer. He left Pavlova in the 1920s to devote full time to painting and is perhaps best known for his paintings of Oriental craftsmen. Stowitts executed a portrait of Mussolini, posed at the Chighi Palace in Rome, probably in the 1930s, and it may be that Pound met Stowitts at that time.

12. Pound contributed (often anonymously) to Dallam Flynn's *Four Pages*. In the third number (March 1948) there appeared the following:

> Difficulties of transport during the plague years led some Canadians to print a number of books in French. The most interesting feature of their list, is the omission of:
>
> | | | | |
> |---|---|---|---|
> | Cocteau | Corbiere | Stendhal | De Gourmont |
> | Gautier | Flaubert | Tailhade | Rene Crevel |

13. *The Little Review*, edited by Margaret Anderson and Jane Heap, was published from 1914 to 1929. Pound was its foreign editor from 1917 to 1921.

14. Probably Princess Troubetzkoi, a Russian émigré in Rome working for the Italian Press and Radio.

15. Philip Mazzei (1730–1816) was a friend of Jefferson's and an active supporter of the American Revolution. From 1779 to 1783 he was an agent of Virginia to secure arms in Italy. Mazzei wrote a four-volume history of the United States and also left his memoirs. It is not clear from Olson's text what Pound was suggesting Olson do an introduction to, but it may have been Howard Marraro's translation of the *Memoirs*. Splavin is George T. Slavin, then of East Providence, R.I., otherwise not yet identified.

16. "West," a long work on the American West, was never written. (Not *West* [London, 1966].)

17. In an undated letter to Olson, his friend "Arioste" (James L. Finlay ?) explained it this way: "The best memory . . . the best memory— The next evening some people showed me two reproductions of french maps 1782: N. & S. America as 'Monde Occidentale' & Europe Africa Asia as

'Monde Orientale';—the best memory in the Orient!" See Olson's use of Pound's lament in "To Gerhardt . . . ," stanza beginning "Admitting that among the ruins."

18. "Ezra Pound on Gold, War, and National Money," *The Capitol Daily*, Washington, D.C., May 9, 1939.

19. Constantin Brancusi (1876–1957), Rumanian born sculptor, often called "the father of modern sculpture." Pound met Brancusi in 1921 in Paris, where Brancusi had lived since 1904. See Pound's essay "Brancusi," written in 1921, in *Literary Essays of Ezra Pound* (New York, 1954).

20. See *Call Me Ishmael* (New York, 1947).

21. *Oro e lavoro*. The first edition, published in 1944, was withdrawn by the printer soon after publication, probably because of Pound's excesses in thought and language.

22. Douglas Goldring (1887–1960) was Ford's assistant editor of the *English Review*. Pound had been reading *South Lodge*, Goldring's reminiscences of Violet Hunt, Ford, and the *English Review* circle. In 1949 Goldring published *Trained for Genius: The Life and Writings of Ford Madox Ford* (New York).

Canto 8

1. Joe Gould (1889?–1957), whom Pound called "that still more unreceived and uncomprehended native hickory," was a Greenwich Village character whose fame rested primarily on his legendary work, "An Oral History of Our Time." For an account of the man and the "Oral History," see Joseph Mitchell, *Joe Gould's Secret* (New York, 1965). Pound had published a small bit of the "Oral History" in *The Exile* (Autumn 1927). I don't know whether Olson was aware of Gould's claim that the "Oral History" had been born of his reading of Yeats ("The history of a nation is not in parliaments and battlefields, but in what the people say to each other on fair days and high days, and in how they farm, and quarrel, and go on pilgrimage"), but his quoting both Gould and Yeats, one after the other, is suggestive.

2. Yeats's poem is entitled "To a Poet, Who Would Have Me Praise Certain Bad Poets, Imitators of His and Mine."

3. In 1949 Fielding Dawson, a student of Olson's at Black Mountain College, wrote that Olson, responding to Dawson's question as to why Olson did not like Sholem Asch, "bent over and rested his elbow on my shoulder,

inhaled a tremendous drag on his cigarette, winked at me and said, 'Every dog has his own fleas.' " Dawson continued, "He likes Ezra Pound very much." *Olson: The Journal of the Charles Olson Archives*, no. 2 (Fall 1974). Olson himself was labeled one of Pound's fleas by Michael Reck in *Ezra Pound: A Close-Up* (London, 1968). And so it goes.

4. F. O. Matthiessen, professor of literature at Harvard and a publisher's reader of *Call Me Ishmael*, turned down the book. See D. G. Bridson, "An Interview with Ezra Pound," *New Directions 17* (1961): 163–64.

5. Janice Biala, artist from New York City.

6. *The Harvard Wake*, no. 5 (Spring 1946).

7. "If T. W. [sic] Hulme's latest editor hasn't quoted it I should like to conserve his 'All a man ever thought would go onto a half sheet of note-paper. The rest is application and elaboration.' " Pound, *Guide to Kulchur* (Norfolk, [1952]) p. 369. Thomas Ernest Hulme (1883–1917) was an English philosopher with a strong interest in aesthetics. Pound included Hulme's "complete poetical works" in *Ripostes*, published in 1912.

Canto 9

1. *Wake* did not devote an issue to Pound. This may account for Pound's coolness to Spencer on his visit to Pound early in 1949. See Noel Stock, *The Life of Ezra Pound* (New York, 1970), p. 427.

2. "The Jolly Corner" appeared in the first number of Ford's *English Review* (December 1908).

3. Walter Winchell (1892–1972) was a gossip columnist and radio commentator who had a rather nasal voice and a strident delivery. He was an early hater of the Nazis (whom he called "Ratzis") and a strong supporter of Roosevelt's.

4. " 'the awfulness that engulfs one when one comes, for the first time unexpectedly on a pile of all the *Murkhn* magazines laid, shinglewise, on a brass-studded, screwed-into-place, baize-covered steamer table. The first glitter of the national weapons for driving off quiet and all closer signs of intelligence.' " Stock, *Life*, p. 87.

5. In "Patria Mia," first published in London in *The New Age*, November 14, 1912.

6. "The Island of Paris: A Letter," *The Dial* 69 (October, November, December 1920).

7. The film was a newsreel of Hitler's visit with Mussolini in 1938. In honor of the occasion, the fleet of Italian submarines, positioned 100 feet apart, dived and surfaced simultaneously. Neither the director of the film nor Pound's review has been identified.

Canto 10

1. Eliot was awarded the Order of Merit on January 1, 1948. The O.M. does not confer knighthood.
2. Pound here is referring to Eliot's failure to examine Milton's *Areopagitica* as he did Milton's verse. Simpson's magazine, *Four Pages*, published in Galveston, Texas, in 1948, by Dallam Simpson (sometimes known as Dallam Flynn) published Williams' article "With Forced Fingers Rude" in the February 1948 issue. Williams states that "Milton's poems . . . remain dangerous reading today for the young writer," Eliot's recanting of Milton as a "bad influence" notwithstanding.
3. Eliot was awarded the Nobel Prize in December 1948.
4. The O.M. was created in 1902. James received it in 1916 from Lord Bryce, who was requested by King George V to deliver it to James on his sickbed. For differing versions of the ceremony, see Leon Edel, *Henry James, the Master: 1901–1916* (New York, 1971), and H. Montgomery Hyde, *Henry James at Home* (London, 1969).
5. Frank Ledlie Moore.
6. Lincoln Kirstein, founder and editor of *The Hound and Horn*, and later a major force in the development of the American ballet.
7. Horn of Plenty probably refers to Kirstein, whose financial support was critical to *The Hound and Horn*.
8. George Leite was editor of *New Rejections* (published in Berkeley, 1941–1943) and *Circle* (published in Berkeley, 1944–1948).
9. "At the root of all intellectual antisemitism is the laodicean serpent that hungers for the Jew's liver." Letter to Olson from Edward Dahlberg, April 21, 1947.
10. Olson went to the West Coast in July 1947. During his stay he was called in as a consultant for John Huston's film *Moby Dick*. Huston's story concerns a huge mechanical whale (built by Jack Warner for his abortive "Moby Dick") which, when launched, sank to the bottom of the tank. Thus whenever Warner heard the words "Moby Dick," his response

was, simply, "That fucking whale." (As reported by Constance Bunker in a conversation with Catherine Seelye.)
11. West Coast poets Robert Duncan, William Everson (Brother Antoninus), Mary Fabilli, Kenneth Rexroth.
12. James L. Finlay?
13. A small town south of San Francisco on Highway 1.

GrandPa, GoodBye

1. Robert Lowell, who was in Washington in 1947–1948 as Consultant in Poetry at the Library of Congress.
2. The following poem (written by Olson probably in 1946) was used as the body of a letter to Pound, which closed with "Will be over Tuesday." Pound acknowledged with "OK."

AUCTOUR

Said the Man of Word, in lated tribute to Good Ford:
"In gratitude for, your Grace and dispensations
I weep coarse thanks, of the living to the dead"

Said Pound the Red, one turquoise earring at his head
"FMF knew more than any of us, he. . . .
from the literary centre, 12 years start of me"

Say I: the Dropsical Man, with beauté in his eye
An Ancient thing, some lumped Raftery
To play the Heart at court of a King

The Dressing Gown, with breath behind the word.
Himself his acre, green island in the modern sea.
Presiding on Fifth Ave.—with new Les Amis.

O Generous Crotchet, with song along the prose
O Fifth Queen Crowned—with a cup of tea:

a writinge man in his lone glorye

3. Pound first credited Ford with the proposition in 1914 when he wrote, "I cannot belittle my belief that Mr. Hueffer's realization that poetry

should be written at least as well as prose," in a review ("Mr. Hueffer and the Prose Tradition in Verse," *Poetry*, 4, no. 3 [June 1914]: 115) of Ford's *Collected Poems*. Ford's belief that poetry must be divested of its "literary" qualities was expressed by him in an essay published as the Preface to his *Collected Poems*.

4. See Williams' essay "Excerpts from a Critical Sketch: A Draft of XXX Cantos by Ezra Pound," in *Selected Essays of William Carlos Williams* (New York, 1954), in which he refers to Pound's "fine ear"; and *The Autobiography of William Carlos Williams* (New York, 1951), p. 225, where he says, "A man with an ear such as his, attuned to the metrical subtleties of the best in verse. . . ." Williams continued to praise Pound's competence even when he was disturbed by the "callousness" of Pound's political views. See his statement that Pound "possessed . . . the most acute ear for metrical sequences, to the point of genius, that we have ever known," in Charles Norman's *The Case of Ezra Pound* (New York, 1968), p. 84. It took Olson to say "that the great 'ear / can no longer 'hear!" in "I, Mencius, Pupil of the Master . . . ," a sentiment he did not long retain.

5. Francis Picabia (1879–1953), French painter, early Dadaist, later developing a highly personal and imaginative style. Gerhart Hauptmann (1862–1946), German dramatist, exponent of the school of naturalism.

6. Pound's first version of Canto I (revised several times after its appearance in *Poetry* 10, no. 3 [June 1917]: 113) is as follows: "Hang it all, there can be but one *Sordello!* / But say I want to, say I take your whole bag / of tricks / Let in your quirks and tweeks, and say the / thing's an art-form, / Your *Sordello*, and that the modern world / Needs such a rag-bag to stuff all its thought in." Fifty years later he said: " 'I picked out this and that thing that interested me, and then jumbled them into a bag. But that's not the way to make'—and here he paused for a moment —'a *work of art.*' " Daniel Cory, "Ezra Pound: A Memoir," *Encounter* 30, no. 5 (1968): 38.

7. Dahlberg writes, "The Western man of ennui is the heir of the fat dregs of Hamlet's sexual sickness. 'O God! I could be bounded in a nutshell . . . were it not that I have bad dreams' is the malady of boredom of the European, of Pascal, Dostoevski, Tolstoi, Stendhal," in *Can These Bones Live* (Norfolk, Conn., 1960), p. 156. In the same essays are found, "At the nethermost core of history, and at the underside of war and poverty, lies tedium. It is the grand malaise of the Western world" (p. 21), and "Thoreau . . . erected in *Walden* the Western Fable of Ennui" (p. 127).

8. "He who knows others is learned, he who knows himself is wise," *The*

Wisdom of Laotse, trans. and ed. by Lin Yutang (New York, [1948]), p. 199.

9. "Cino" was first published in *A lume spento* in 1908.

10. See Robert Grosseteste, *On Light* (Milwaukee, 1942), and Carroll F. Terrell, "A Commentary on Grosseteste . . . ," *Paideuma* 2, no. 3 (Winter 1973) : 449–70.

11. They are in "Paradiso." Eliot's images of light to which Olson refers are probably those in "Burnt Norton" or possibly those in "Choruses from 'The Rock.' "

12. "The Nun's Priest's Tale." (Text from F. N. Robinson's *The Works of Geoffrey Chaucer,* 2nd ed. [Boston, 1957], p. 242.)

13. Guy Davenport, in "Pound and Frobenius," *Motive and Method in The Cantos of Ezra Pound,* ed. by Lewis Leary (New York, 1954), p. 36, reports that the title page will bear "three emblems, the Chinese character for sincerity . . . and two prehistoric African rock figures of hunters, from drawings made by Frobenius."

14. Pound is probably referring to his essay "The Serious Artist," first published in *The New Freewoman* (October-November 1913), republished in *Pavannes and Divisions* (1918).

15. Olson sent Williams a copy of "GrandPa, GoodBye." Williams responded as follows:

> Friday night [1948]
>
> Dear Chas:
>
> This thing (GrandPa : GoodBye) on ol' Ez makes you one of the few men I take pleasure in reading. It is fresh as a field of hay— and it's dangerous to talk that way—but it gives me that feeling. As always it's the style. But the style reveals the mind. So it's the mind. It's got what if I live long enough I'll finally live for nothing else. It's got the bloom of the mind on it—that leaves the sense intact.
>
> I like it very much—quite for what it says and not just for you.
>
> Send it out, there's nothing like it around here. It will stand out like an arm—if they'll print it. They won't dare. They're all too God damned CLEAN. Sickening.
>
> Something's got to bust around here soon. I wish I knew how to bring it about. Something's got to out-step the big army smash-up or it really *will* get us. Always this approach to a break through in the arts coming JUST before our presence becomes intollerable [*sic*] to the money boys and the blood has to spill.

I've been noticing myself recently, how repulsive the faces about me on the street have become—and numerous. Not the poor. They at least have a beauty. But the money guys, the little money guys. They are getting dominant again and they are ugly, ugly as hell. And they're everywhere.

Won't Karl Shapiro (poor guy) put it in Poetry? Or if you want to go to the trouble of making half a dozen copies send it to—

Marguerite Caetani	Poetry: New York
Princess di Bassiano	14 Avenue A
Via Botteghe Oscure #32	New York 9
Rome, Italy	N.Y.

Why not try John Crowe Ransom? Partisan Review. (Shove it FAR up their asses) They ought to print it but they won't.

I return it to you with my blessing. I hope you're over your cold.

Best

[signed: Bill]

16. Thomas Sturge Moore (1870–1944), English poet and artist.

17. Pound had said earlier of *Call Me Ishmael*, "I read with joy—made it unnecessary to read Melville."

18. Hugh Kenner reports that when Frobenius and Pound met, "each was astonished by his physical resemblance to the other." *The Pound Era* (Berkeley, 1971), p. 507.

19. Agnes Bedford, a musician who collaborated with Pound on *Five Troubadour Songs*. She later helped Pound with technical matters when he began to compose operas.

20. Olson uses this sentiment three years later in "Letter for Melville": "a very great man, said / of another—who never learned a thing / from Melville—worth / 'five Oxfords on ten thousand Cambridges'!"

21. Pound told Olson on another occasion that Joyce was referring to *Hugh Selwyn Mauberley*. The fifth line of "Medallion" reads, "The sleek head emerges."

22. The play in question here is *Michael Kramer*. See *Letters of James Joyce*, 3 vols. (New York, 1966), 1:398; 3:415. Joyce also translated Hauptmann's *Vor Sonnenaufgang*.

23. Olson might have been less derisive had he known of Eliot's financial position: "I recall that a number of years ago when I had less money than I have now, if I was in New York and wanted to go down to St. Elizabeth's [sic] Hospital in Washington to see Ezra Pound, I had to

manage somehow to get a date to read in order to foot the bill!' " William Levy, *Affectionately, T. S. Eliot* . . . (Philadelphia, 1968), p. 64.

24. "For three years, out of key with his time, / He strove to resuscitate the dead art / Of poetry; to maintain 'the sublime' / In the old sense. Wrong from the start—" Pound, *Hugh Selwyn Mauberley*.

Appendix

1. Elsie Martindale was Ford Madox Ford's legal wife. After an unsuccessful attempt to divorce her in Giessen, Germany, where he "resumed" his German citizenship for this purpose, Ford lived successively with Violet Hunt, Stella Bowen, and Janice Biala.

2. Arthur Waley (1889–1966), a well-known sinologist and translator of Chinese and Japanese literature. He was born Arthur David Schloss. Waley and Pound were friends in Pound's London years. In 1963 Waley said of that relationship, ". . . what he [Pound] said about poetry and this business of making poetry is much the best that I've ever heard said in the course of my life." "Arthur Waley in Conversation: BBC Interview with Roy Fuller (1963)," in *Madly Singing in the Mountains*, ed., Ivan Morris, (New York, 1970), p. 140.

3. Eliot was editor of the *Criterion*, which published "the poetry and fiction of D. H. Lawrence, Hart Crane, and others, paying attention to European writers, neglecting many important Americans." Frederick J. Hoffman, *The Little Magazine* (Princeton, N.J., 1947), p. 386.

4. "Russia to the Pacifists" in *The Years Between* (New York, 1919), pp. 43–45.

5. The Greenback party (or the Independent party) was formed in 1874 by farmers and died before the end of the century. The party advocated the continuing withdrawal of all bank currency to be replaced entirely by government issued paper money, or "greenbacks." Pound felt the doctrine to be sound but the method evil: paper money still in circulation could not be used for the payment of the national debt or for import duties, a restriction that ultimately played into the hands of the banks which still held the nation's gold. In 1958 Pound was still calling for "some of the sanity of the Greenback Party." Charles Norman, *The Case of Ezra Pound* (New York, 1968), p. 199.

6. Theodore Lothrup Stoddard (1883–1950), a prolific writer with a strong

belief in Nordic supremacy. "Capitol Times" should be read *The Capitol Daily*, a newssheet published in Washington from October 1937 to June 1939. Pound's article "Ezra Pound on Gold, War, and Money" appeared on the front page of the final issue (a development not uncommon to Pound, who often appeared in final issues). Stoddard's name appears in these records twice in connection with *The Capitol Daily*, but his association with the paper has not yet been established.

7. Sir Oswald Mosley, British politician, founder of the New Party and leader of the British Union of Fascists, the latter noted for its campaign against the Jews. Pound contributed to Mosley's *Fascist Quarterly*, the *British Union Quarterly*, and *Action*, and Mosley's Greater British Publications brought out Pound's *What Is Money For?* (1939).

8. Possibly R. Rinoni, an official for the Italian Press and Radio.

9. Conte Galeazzo Ciano (1903–1944), Mussolini's Foreign Minister and husband of Mussolini's daughter Edda. Mussolini had Ciano shot for his participation in Mussolini's defeat in 1943 by the Grand Council.

10. Olga Rudge.

11. Ernest Francisco Fenollosa (1853–1908), American orientalist from whose papers Pound, as literary executor, published *Cathay* (1915), *Certain Noble Plays of Japan* (1916), and *"Noh" or Accomplishment* (1917). Fenollosa was buried in Japan, where he had been Imperial Commissioner of Art.

12. Briarcliffe is *Briarcliffe Quarterly*, published by Briarcliffe Junior College from 1944 to 1947 under the editorship of Norman Macleod. Its January 1947 issue was devoted to contemporary Italian literature. J. P. Angold, English poet and writer on economics, appearing primarily in *New English Weekly*, was killed in World War II. Olson, as an emissary of Pound's, was attempting to place some of Angold's unpublished (?) poetry in American magazines. Rupert Brooke (1887–1915) was a very popular romantic poet who was killed in World War I. Although Pound wrote to Harriet Monroe that Brooke "was the best of all that Georgian group," Pound was criticized for a poem, "Our Contemporaries," which appeared in *Blast* soon after Brooke's death, a poem which some saw as an attack on Brooke.

13. George Santayana (1863–1952), American philosopher whom Pound met in Rome in 1939.

14. Laurence Binyon (1869–1943), English poet, dramatist, and art critic. Pound is referring to Binyon's translation of Dante.

15. Probably Harriet Monroe (1861?–1936) of *Poetry*, Margaret Anderson (1890?–1973) of *The Little Review*, and Marianne Moore (1887–1972)

of *The Dial.* Margaret Anderson published a blank issue, except for drawings in the center fold, of *The Little Review* (vol. 12, no. 2). "Since no art was being produced we would make no attempt to publish any." Anderson, *My Thirty Years' War* (New York, 1970), p. 124.

16. In June 1946 Italy voted 54 percent to 46 percent in favor of a republic. Trieste and the immediate vicinity around it were made a free territory after the war, occupied by both Anglo-American and Yugoslav troops. Russia, during this period, was pressing Yugoslavia's claims to the whole of Trieste.

17. Archibald MacLeish, "Victory Without Peace," *Saturday Review of Literature* 29, no. 6 (February 9, 1946): 5–7.

18. Pound is probably referring to *Prufrock and Other Observations*, published in 1917. Pound persuaded Harriet Weaver "to lend him the Egoist imprint if he would raise enough money to cover the cost of printing." Noel Stock, *The Life of Ezra Pound* (New York, 1970), pp. 204–05.

19. Pound had suggested that Olson might take on Omar's education and Dorothy Pound urged Olson to do so. She had acknowledged that Ezra found Olson's visits very stimulating and that Omar had reported that he was learning a great deal from just listening to Olson. Olson's response is not known.

20. Although Pound was a federal prisoner, he was confined briefly in the District of Columbia jail and was under the jurisdiction of Howard B. Gill, Superintendent of Prisons for the District of Columbia. It was Gill who authorized the release of *The Pisan Cantos* and *Confucius* to New Directions after the Federal Bureau of Prisons had denied Pound permission to turn them over for publication. Gill continued to visit Pound after his transfer to St. Elizabeths, as a "friendly visitor." Letter to Catherine Seelye from Howard B. Gill, November 29, 1973. James Legge (1815–1897), Confucian scholar and a missionary to China, found Confucian thought and principles antagonistic to Christianity.

21. The four books are the Confucian quartet: *The Analects, The Great Learning, The Doctrine of the Mean,* and *The Works of Mencius.*

22. Gabriele D'Annunzio (1863–1938), Italian poet, playwright, novelist, propagandist, and ardent soldier.

23. Henry Crowder was a Black American jazz musician who met Nancy Cunard in Paris in the 1920s. Crowder lived in Washington after World War II. Miss Cunard reminded Pound in 1946 that "Henry loved you." Pound wrote back, "Wish I had Henry's address." Evidently, he got it. (For these two letters, see Hugh Ford, ed., *Nancy Cunard: Brave Poet, Indomitable Rebel, 1896–1965* [Philadelphia, 1968], pp. 358–61.)

24. Elsie Mackay accompanied Capt. W. G. R. Hinchliffe on his tragic attempt to cross the Atlantic from England to America in 1928. The plane and its occupants were never found.
25. Hilda Doolittle (1886–1961), American poet, one of the early Imagists.
26. John J. Slocum, a Joyce collector (whose library forms the nucleus of the collection at Yale) and compiler (with Herbert Cahoon) of *A Bibliography of James Joyce.* Pound met Slocum through James Laughlin in Austria in 1935; he saw him again in New York in 1939.
27. Henry L. Mencken (1880–1956), American editor, satirist, and literary critic.
28. In 1959 Pound had this to say of Bennett: "I mean we were [in 1911] so aesthetic that Arnold Bennett got on my nerves, and I lost great opportunities—how I would have loved Bennett's conversation when my mind had developed to the point where I could take it in." D. G. Bridson, "An Interview with Ezra Pound," *New Directions 17* (1961): 162.
29. Lewis' novel *Tarr*, which Eliot reviewed in *The Egoist* (September 1918), likening Lewis ("the most fascinating personality of our time") to Dostoevski.
30. I am unaware of Joyce's expression of his debt to Pound "on language." It is not known if Joyce read much (any?) Pound; it is generally accepted that his praise of Pound was restricted to Pound's personal kindnesses.
31. Rabindranath Tagore (1861–1941), Indian poet, dramatist, and novelist whom Yeats helped with English translations of his works.
32. "Medievalism" first appeared in *Guido Cavalcanti Rime* (Genova, [1932]). Olson probably saw the essay in *Make It New.*

Index